THE RIDDLE OF REVELATION

FOCUSING ON THE SEALS, TRUMPETS, & BOWLS

G. Michael Cocoris

© 2025 G. Michael Cocoris

All rights reserved. This publication may not be reproduced (in whole or in part, edited, or revised) in any way, form, or means, including, but not limited to electronic, mechanical, photocopying, recording or any kind of storage and retrieval system *for sale*, except for brief quotations in printed reviews, without the written permission of G. Michael Cocoris, 2016 Euclid #20, Santa Monica, CA 90405, michaelcocoris@gmail.com, or his appointed representatives. Permission is hereby granted, however, for reproduction of the whole or parts of the whole without changing the content in any way for *free distribution,* provided all copies contain this copyright notice in its entirety. Permission is also granted to charge for the cost of copying.

Unless otherwise indicated, all Scripture quotations are taken from the New King James Version ®, Copyright © 1979, 1980, 1982 by Thomas Nelson, Inc. Used by permission. All rights reserve

TABLE OF CONTENTS

Chapter 1	Introduction	1
Chapter 2	Interpretations of Revelation	3
Chapter 3	The Tribulation	12
Chapter 4	An Overview of Revelation	31
Chapter 5	The Seven Seals	45
Chapter 6	The Seven Trumpets	61
Chapter 7	The Explanatory Prophecies	79
Chapter 8	The Seven Bowles	99
Chapter 9	Conclusion	113
Appendix I:	Seals, Trumpets, & Bowls	117
Appendix II:	Matthew 24 And The Seals, Trumpets, & Bowls	123
Bibliopraphy		125
About The Author		129

Chapter 1

INTRODUCTION

The book of Revelation is a riddle! Just look at what it says. Horses are not just white, red, and black; they are also pale (green) (6:4). Twenty-five percent of the people on the planet are killed (6:8). The sun turns black (6:12). The moon turns red (6:12). Stars fall from heaven to earth (6:13). Human suffering is so severe that the survivors cry out for the mountains to fall on them (6:15-16). That is only the beginning!

Hail and fire mingled with blood fall to the earth and a third of all the trees and green grass are burned up (8:7). A burning mountain falls into the ocean and a third of all sea life and a third of all ships are destroyed (8:9). A similar fate happens to the rivers and they become bitter (8:10-11). The sun, the moon, and the stars are so dark that a third of each day is darkness (8:12). Supernatural locusts ascend from a bottomless pit to torment people for five months but do not kill them (9:1-6). As if enough damage has not been done already, another third of the population is killed (9:13-21). That means that 50% of the people on the earth have now been destroyed. If the earth's population were 100 and one-fourth died, 75 people would be left. Then, if one-third of those died, 50 would be left. But the end has not yet come.

The Riddle of Revelation

A dragon has seven heads and ten horns (12:3). A woman is given two wings of an eagle (12:14). A beast with seven heads and ten horns comes out of the sea (13:1). There is more, much more, but you get the picture. The book of Revelation is a riddle!

What in the world is going on? No doubt this is symbolic language, but symbols have significance. What is the significance of the symbols in the book of Revelation? The significance is a much-debated subject. Several different issues need to be addressed to unravel the riddle.

First, what are the different interpretations of the book? Which one is correct?

Second, taken at face value, the book seems to suggest that there will be a time of great trouble before the Second Coming of Christ. Bible teachers refer to such a period as "the Tribulation." What does the Bible say about the Tribulation? How long is it? Apart from the book of Revelation, what is known about it?

Third, what can be learned from the book's text about what it is saying? The layout or structure of the book is critical. An overview of the book as a whole would help explain the details of the book.

Finally, one of the most difficult problems in the book of Revelation is determining the structure of the three series of seven judgments: the seal, trumpet, and bowl judgments. What is the solution to that part of the puzzle?

Let's explore each of these issues. When that is done, The Riddle of Revelation will be solved.

Chapter 2

INTERPRETATIONS OF REVELATION

Throughout history, the book of Revelation has been interpreted in various ways. In a sense, the major approaches to interpreting Revelation revolve around the concept of time. Some say the book was fulfilled in the past, either in the first century or throughout the centuries. Others claim it will be fulfilled just before Christ returns. Then, some contend that time is not the issue. The following four interpretations have been the most prominent.

The Idealist View

Explanation Basically, this theory maintains that there are only a few, if any, references to any time, including the first century or otherwise. Revelation is not about the first century, history, or the future. It is about ideas and principles (Morris, p. 20).

This approach originated with Clement of Alexandria (ca. 150-ca. 215) and Origen (185-254). They regarded the book of Revelation "as one great allegory going far beyond the natural symbolism" (Walvoord, p. 16). Thiessen states, "They allegorized everything they could not understand and also much that they could" (Thiessen, p. 324).

Augustine (354-430) adopted a modified form of allegorical interpretation. He saw Revelation as a symbolic way of presenting the conflict between Christianity and evil, a conflict between the City of God and the City of Satan (Walvoord, p. 17).

A modern form of this view teaches that Revelation contains general principles concerning the conflict between the church and evil. Milligan says, "These successive waves of judgment are obviously successive in thought rather than time" (Milligan, p. 148). He claims that Revelation is "not a history of either early or medieval or last events written before they happened, but a spring of elevating encouragement and holy joy to Christians in every age" (Milligan, p. 155).

Evaluation This method of interpretation requires extensive allegorization, which entirely disregards the book's plain statements. According to Thiessen, this position "overlooks the fact that the book claims to be a prophecy (1:3; 10:11; 22:7, 10, 18, 19) and that it points to the second advent (1:7; 3:11; 16:15; 19:7; 22:7, 12, 20)" (Thiessen, p. 324).

The Preterist View

Explanation According to this view, John wrote about the first-century situation and had nothing more in mind than that. Revelation begins with the first-century church and ends there (Morris, p. 18). It concerns "nothing further than the destruction of pagan and persecuting Rome" (Alford, vol. IV, p. 246). This school of thought includes those who say the major prophecies

Interpretations of Revelation

were fulfilled in the fall of Jerusalem (AD 70) or Rome (AD 476; Mounce, p. 41). Either way, it is symbolic history rather than prophecy. It is descriptive, not predictive (Walvoord, p. 17). The Jesuit Alcazar (d. 1614), "a thoroughgoing preterist," was the first to interpret chapters 4-19 as being fulfilled in the first century and the centuries immediately following (Mounce, p. 41).

A modern commentator says, "The Apocalypse is a book of its time, written out of its time and for its time, not for the distant generations of the future or even of the end-time" (Kummel, cited by Morris, fn., p. 19).

Evaluation Like the Idealist view, this notion exercises extensive allegorization, entirely ignoring the book's plain statements.

A pastor friend, who said he was leaning toward this explanation, told me that the book was fulfilled in the reign of Nero (AD 54-68) and the destruction of Jerusalem (AD 70). For example, his interpretation of hail was that it consisted of white stones that resembled hail, which the Romans hurled at Jerusalem. He admitted, however, that if the book was written in AD 95, this interpretation could not be sustained.

What is the date for the writing of Revelation? There are two theories. The early date claims it was written during the reign of Nero, about AD 68 or 69. The late date contends it was penned during the reign of Domitian, about AD 95 or 96.

To a large degree, the early date is based on the interpretation that the statement, "There are also seven kings. Five have fallen, one is, *and* the other has not yet come" (17:10), refers to the

Roman emperors. Even the proponents of this position cannot agree on which emperors fit this description. All explanations are speculation. Those who begin the count with Julius Caesar date the book in the reign of Nero (Moses Stuart). Those who begin with Augustus date the book in the reign of Galba (Ewald); or, if Galba, Otho, and Vitellius (who had only about a year between them) are counted as usurpers, the date is in the reign of Vespasian (Eichhorn; Bleek). In other words, dating the book based on that interpretation of Revelation 17:10 is arbitrary. There is no solid evidence for the early date of the writing of Revelation—only guesses.

Hort, who argues for a date in Nero's time, admits that the Domitian view (Revelation was written in AD 95) is the "prevalent tradition" that "goes back to an author likely to be the recipient of a true tradition on the matter." He even concedes, "If external evidence alone could decide, there would be a clear preponderance for Domitian."

Reasons for the late date include: 1) Since John did not move to Ephesus until AD 67, the early date would not give him enough time to establish an ongoing ministry in Asia by the time he wrote this book. 2) The churches described in chapters 2 and 3 were founded in the late 50s. The early date allows too little time for the decline described to develop (2:4; 3:1, 15-18). 3) The deeds of Domitian were more relevant than those of Nero. 4) Tradition.

Irenaeus (130-202), a disciple of Polycarp (ca. 70-155), who was a disciple of John, says, "For it was seen, not long ago, but almost in our generation, near the end of Domitian's reign

(Irenaeus, *Adv. Hoer.* v. 30.3; ii. 22.5; iii. 4.4). Clement of Alexandria (ca. 150-ca. 220) and Eusebius (ca. 265-ca. 339) do not name Domitian, but they no doubt have him in mind. Victorinus (270-303) says Domitian condemned John to the mines in Patmos. Jerome (ca. 347-420) says that John saw the Apocalypse in Patmos, where Domitian had banished him.

Domitian was the first emperor to demand emperor worship while he was alive. That led to persecution (Barclay, vol. 2, p. 182). The Domitian type of persecution best fits the situation described in Revelation chapters 2-3.

The preterists who extend the events of the book beyond 70 to 476 do not eliminate all the problems. "The major problem with the preterist position is that the decisive victory portrayed in the latter chapters of the Apocalypse was never achieved. It is difficult to believe that John envisioned anything less than the complete overthrow of Satan, the final destruction of evil, and the eternal reign of God" (Mounce, pp. 41-42).

The Historical View

Explanation: This approach views the book as a continuous history spanning from the first century to the consummation. Alford points out, "In early times, the historic material since the apostolic period was not copious enough to tempt man to fit it onto the symbols of the prophetic visions" (Alford, vol. IV, p. 246). Berengaud (9th century) was the first to suggest this approach, but Joachim (1150) popularized it in the 12th century. Many in the Reformed tradiyion viewed the book as a judgment, not just against pagans, but also against the papal Roman Church. The Antichrist sits on the throne of the papacy (Alford, vol. IV, p. 246). Advocates of this approach include Wycliffe, Luther, Sir Isaac Newton, Bengel, Bullinger, Barnes, and Alford (Alford, vol. IV, p. 247; Thiessen, p. 325). Lange, a modern commentator, "holds that the seals, trumpets, and vials are a symbolic presentation of the whole of human history" (Walvoord, p. 124).

Evaluation This interpretation is subjective. Proponents cannot agree on whether this or that king or this or that pope is intended, or whether the text refers to a past persecution or one yet to come (Kuyper, cited by Walvoord, p. 19). There is no objective standard to determine which historical fulfillment is accurate.

This view "breeds uncertainty and confusion" (Kuyper, cited by Walvoord, p. 20). Walvoord says, "At least fifty different systems of interpretation have arisen from the historical view alone" (Walvoord, p. 125) and, "Many of the historical interpretations have already been proved false by historical developments" (Walvoord, p. 125).

In the words of Morris, it labors "under the serious disadvantage of failing to agree. If the main points of subsequent history are, in fact, foreshadowed, it should be possible to identify them with tolerable certainty; otherwise, what is the point of it? But there are many historicist views and no real agreement" (Morris, p. 19). Walvoord puts it this way: "The very multiplicity of such interpretations and identifications of the personnel of Revelation with a variety of historical characters is its own reputation. If the

Interpretations of Revelation

historical method is correct, it is clear that until now no one has found the key" (Walvoord, p. 19).

The Futurist View

Explanation: This explanation states that Chapter 19 is about the Second Coming (19:11-16). So, the events described in chapters 4-18 occur just before the Second Coming. First, a series of seal judgments are revealed (6:1-7). Then trumpet judgments come out of the seal judgments (8:1-2) and the bowl judgments are the last plagues (15:1). The trumpets cover the 3½ years (11:2, 3; 12:6, 14; 13:5) just before the Second Coming (11:15). Therefore, the futurist view is correct.

The futurist view was the original view. Alford is emphatic, stating that those who abandoned primitive interpretations of such things as the millennial reign of Christ not only wrestle with the plain sense of words but "desert the unanimous consensus of the primitive fathers, some of whom lived early enough to have retained apostolic tradition on this point" (Alford, vol. IV, p. 252). Proponents of this position include Irenaeus, Theodoret, Gregory the Great, and Tertullian. It is the basic view of Pre-millennialists.

Evaluation: The major criticism of this point of view is that it offers little comfort to first-century believers facing persecution (Mounce, pp. 42-43). That criticism is not legitimate. The nature of biblical prophecy is that distant events have an immediate application (2 Pet. 3:10-14). As Mounce says, "This age will come to an end and Satan and his host will be destroyed and the righteous will be vindicated. These are historical events, which will take place in time. And they are future" (Mounce, p. 44). He adds, "It is the end that gives meaning to the process" (Mounce, p. 44).

Summary: The book of Revelation reveals what will happen just before Christ's coming, not general principles for all time, nor what happened in the first century or during church history.

There are other methods of interpretation. Some combine two of the methods mentioned, but the method of interpretation that takes the book at face value has to conclude that the fulfillment of the prophecy in the book is still in the future.

Therefore, chapters 2-3 contain letters to seven historic churches in the first century. Chapters 4-18 describe events just before the Second Coming. Chapter 19 depicts the Second Coming, and chapters 20-22 reveal what will happen after the Second Coming.

Originally, the book of Revelation was not intended to be a riddle. The very opposite is the case. The book opens with "The Revelation of Jesus Christ" (1:1). The Greek word translated as "revelation" is a compound word composed of two words: "from" and "cover, veil, conceal." It means "an uncovering, a revealing." The picture embedded in the word is that of taking the veil away, removing the veil, or unveiling. This book was not meant to conceal but to reveal. It was not intended to confuse but to clarify.

The book may strike first-time readers as unusual because it contains graphic symbols. A careful reading resolves most of

Interpretations of Revelation

those problems. Symbols have significance. In the case of Revelation, the symbols are often explained. For example, in chapter 1, the lampstands (1:12) and the stars (1:16) are explained (1:20).

Commentators create confusion by forcing the book into a specific period, such as the first century, or by ignoring all references to time. Taken at face value, it is apparent that the book of Revelation is a revealing of Jesus Christ as judge of the church (chapters 2-3) and the world (chapters 4-18) and as coming King (chapters 20-22; see 1:5). Jesus Christ will punish the wicked world and reward the faithful.

Chapter 3
THE TRIBULATION

The prophecies in the book of Revelation are *not* about the first century, all of church history, or principles for all time. Most of Revelation (chapters 4-18) describes a period just before the Second Coming of Christ (chapter 19). Understanding that much of the book resolves a large part of The Riddle of Revelation, but it does not solve the entire riddle. Being aware that chapters 4-18 portray a period just before the coming of Christ does not answer several critical questions posed by those chapters. Revelation 4-18 contains three sets of seven judgments: the seal judgments (4:1-8:2), the trumpet judgments (8:3-11:19), and the bowl judgments (15:1-16:21). How are they related to the period just before the coming of Christ?

Usually, the questions of interpretation raised by a book of the Bible are answered from information gleaned from the book itself; if not in the immediate context, then within the context of the book. There are, however, cases when it is necessary to look beyond a biblical book to understand an interpretive problem within it. For example, in 2 Corinthians, Paul refers to a situation at Corinth that he does not explain in 2 Corinthians (2 Cor. 2:5-11). Many students of 2 Corinthians have concluded that insight into the problem mentioned in 2 Corinthians is best obtained from

1 Corinthians (1 Cor. 5:1-13).

That is true concerning the judgments before the Second Coming recorded in Revelation 4-18. Numerous passages in the Bible refer to a period preceding the coming of Christ, often called the "Tribulation." Understanding several of these passages will help in answering questions raised by Revelation 4-18, especially the relationship between the judgments in Revelation 4-18 and the Tribulation.

Think of Revelation as the last chapter in a long book. Does it not make sense that knowing what the book says before the last chapter would help the reader better understand the final chapter? Likewise, knowing what the Bible says about the time just before the kingdom helps explain Revelation 4-18.

Of all the passages in the Bible that speak about the time just before the kingdom, two are particularly important in understanding Revelation: Daniel 9 and Mathew 24. Although they both discuss the same topics, Matthew 24 even refers to Daniel 9, Matthew 24 is of the utmost importance. In the nineteenth century, Dean Henry Alford, an Englishman who wrote a commentary on the entire Greek New Testament, stated that the first great key to understanding the book of Revelation is Old Testament prophecy, and the next is the Lord's prophetic discourse in Matthew 24 (Alford, vol. IV, p. 253).

Alford also said, "The close connection between our Lord's prophetic discourse on the Mount of Olives, and the line of apocalyptic prophecy, cannot fail to have struck every student of Scripture" (Alford, vol. IV, p. 249). Matthew 24 has been called "the anchor of apocalyptic interpretation" (Williams, cited by Alford, vol. IV, p. 249), "the touchstone of apocalyptic systems" (Alford, vol. IV, p. 249). Alford goes so far as to say that if the guidance of Matthew 24 is not followed in interpreting the seals, the true key to the book of Revelation is lost (Alford, vol. IV, p. 249). What do Daniel 9 and Matthew 24 say that helps explain Revelation?

Daniel 9

The Prayer Jeremiah predicted that the captivity of the Jews would last seventy years (Jer. 25:11-12, 29:10-14). After spending years in Babylon, Daniel realized he was living on the threshold of fulfilling Jeremiah's prophecy (Dan. 9:1-2). So, Daniel prayed for the restoration of Jerusalem (Dan. 9:3-19).

The Program Gabriel told Daniel, "Seventy weeks are determined for your people and for your holy city, to finish the transgression, to make an end of sins, to make reconciliation for iniquity, to bring in everlasting righteousness, to seal up vision and prophecy, and to anoint the Most Holy. Know, therefore, and understand *that* from the going forth of the command to restore and build Jerusalem until Messiah the Prince, *there shall be* seven weeks and sixty-two weeks; the street shall be built again, and the wall, even in troublesome times. And after the sixty-two weeks, the Messiah shall be cut off, but not for Himself; and the people of the prince who is to come shall destroy the city and the sanctuary.

The end of it *shall be* with a flood, and till the end of the war, desolations are determined. Then, he shall confirm a covenant with many for one week, but in the middle of the week, he shall bring an end to sacrifice and offering and on the wing of abominations shall be one who makes desolate, even until the consummation, which is determined, is poured out on the desolate" (Dan 9:24-27).

Gabriel told Daniel, "Seventy weeks are determined for your people and for your holy city" (Dan. 9:24). The Hebrew word translated "weeks" means "sevens" (plural). God's program for Israel and Jerusalem involves not just 70 years but "seventy sevens." The seventy years of captivity discussed earlier in the chapter indicate that Gabriel means "seventy sevens" of years, that is, 490 years. Only "years" makes sense. In fact, 490 days (70 x 7 days) or 490 months (70 x 7 months) is meaningless. Furthermore, 490 years fit what happened (see below).

Thus, Gabriel is saying that God has a program for Israel that encompasses "seventy weeks (sevens)" of years, that is, 490 years (Dan. 9:24). The purpose of this program is to end sin and establish righteousness (Dan. 9:24), that is, establish the kingdom. The concept of a week of years is used elsewhere (Gen. 29:27; see the sabbatical year in Lev. 25; Deut. 15).

According to Daniel 9:25, the beginning of the 490-year program for Israel is marked by the command to restore and rebuild Jerusalem, which is divided into three parts. The first phase is "seven weeks" (49 years). During this period, "the street shall be built again, and the wall, even in troublesome times" (Dan. 9:25).

The Tribulation

The second phase is 69 weeks (7 weeks and 62 weeks, which is 483 years). The Messiah comes after 483 years (Dan. 9:25). The question is, "When was the command to restore and build Jerusalem?" When do the 490 years begin?

There were four commands pertaining to rebuilding. Three deal with the Temple or the wall: the Decree of Cyrus (Ezra 1) in 539 BC, the Decree of Darius (Ezra 6) in 519 BC, the Decree of Artaxerxes (Ezra 7) in 458 BC, and the Decree of Artaxerxes (Neh. 2) in 445 BC. Which one of these is the starting date for the 490 years?

Some distinguished commentators have used the Decree of Cyrus as the starting point (Calvin, Keil, Leupold, Young, et al.). There are two problems with that view. First, Cyrus's Decree was to rebuild the Temple (Ezra 1:2-4). It was not a command "to restore and build Jerusalem," although apparently, the people who returned with Ezra did work on the walls (Ezra 5:9). The second difficulty is that it puts the coming of the Messiah at 56 BC (539 + 483 = 56 BC).

Using the Decree of Darius does not solve either problem associated with the Decree of Cyrus. It only reaffirms the Decree of Cyrus "to build this house of God at Jerusalem" (Ezra 6:3, 7) and it falls short of the coming of Christ (519 + 483 = 33 BC).

At first glance, it seems that the Decree of Artaxerxes also concerned the Temple (Ezra 7:19-20), but it clearly includes much more than that. Artaxerxes says they could do "whatever seems good to you," "according to the will of God" (Ezra 7:18). Later, Ezra thanked God that He "did not forsake us in our bondage; but

He extended mercy to us in the sight of the kings of Persia, to revive us, to repair the house of our God, to rebuild its ruins, and to give us a wall in Judah and Jerusalem" (Ezra 9:9) Moreover, it fits the coming of Christ perfectly.

Calling this the traditional view, Boutflower dates the Decree in AD 457 and concludes that 483 years later, in AD 26, is the year the Messiah was made manifest to Israel (Charles Boutflower, *In and Around The Book of Daniel*, pp. 186-191). Archer also dates the Decree in 457 BC, but he arrives at AD 25 as the time of Christ's ministry (Gleason L. Archer, Jr., *A Survey of the Old Testament Introduction*, p. 387). Wood states that the Decree was issued in 458 BC, and the 483-year period ends in AD 26, as only one year elapsed between 1 BC and AD 1 (Leon Wood, *A Commentary on Daniel*, pp. 252-254).

Because it specifically pertained to the rebuilding of the wall, many have concluded that the commencement of the 483 years is the Decree of Artaxerxes recorded in Nehemiah 2. The problem, of course, is that this starting point places the coming of Christ in 38 AD (445 + 483 = AD 38).

In his book *The Coming Prince*, Sir Robert Anderson says that the 483 years are "prophetic" years of 360 days (Anderson, pp. 67-75; Rev. 11:2-3; 12:6, 14; 13:5), that Christ died on April 6, AD 32 (Anderson, pp. 88-105, 127), and that the Decree was issued on March 3, 445 BC (Anderson, pp. 119-24). He concludes that the phrase "unto Messiah the Prince" was fulfilled on the day of the triumphal entry, Sunday, April 6, AD 32 (Anderson, pp. 127-128). Sixty-nine weeks of prophetic years of 360 days or 69

The Tribulation

x 7 x 360 = 173,880 days. There are 476 years, 24 days between March 14, 445 BC, and April 6, AD 32, plus 116 days for leap years, totaling 173,880 days. Thus, he dates the crucifixion in AD 32. Showers agrees with Anderson (Renald E. Showers, *The Most High God*, pp. 120-125).

Others begin the 70 weeks with the Decree of Artaxerxes recorded in Nehemiah 2, but not all of them arrive at AD 32 for the crucifixion. Walvoord does not commit himself to a date for the crucifixion (Walvoord, pp. 223-228). Hoehner accepts this Decree as the beginning of the 70 weeks but claims the date is 444 BC instead of 445 BC. Therefore, according to him, the crucifixion was in AD 33 (Harold W. Hoehner, *Chronological Aspects of the Life of Christ*, pp. 115-39). Campbell concurs with Hoehner (Donald K. Campbell, *Daniel: Decoder of Dreams*, p.110).

The traditional view that the program began with the Decree of Artaxerxes (Ezra 7) is the best explanation. According to Gabriel, God's future program for Israel began in 458 BC.

Phase One From the Decree of Artaxerxes in 458 BC until the streets and walls were built was 49 years (409 BC). The Hebrew word translated "wall" is not the normal Hebrew word for "wall." It means "to cut." Modern lexicographers render it "ditch, moat." This refers to an aspect of Jerusalem's fortification. The Hebrew word for "street" means "wide space" and refers to a marketplace or public square. In other words, it took 49 years from the Decree to restore Jerusalem as a thriving city.

Phase Two Daniel 9:26 begins with "after 62 weeks." Actually, it is after 69 weeks, which is the sum of the seven weeks in verse

25 and the sixty-two weeks in verse 26, totaling 69 weeks or 483 years. This period begins with the Decree in AD 457 and concludes 483 years later in AD 26 (Boutflower; Wood) or AD 25 (Archer, Jr.).

Two things take place: 1) Daniel 9:26 states that after 69 weeks, the Messiah shall be cut off, but not for Himself. "Cut off" means "to destroy, to kill" (Gen 9:11). 2) Daniel 9:26 says the people of the prince that shall come shall destroy the city and the sanctuary.

The "prince that shall come" is different from the Messiah, the prince. Based on what Daniel 9:27 says he will do and what we know from other passages, this is the Antichrist, but Daniel 9:26 is not talking about the Antichrist. It discusses the people of the Antichrist, specifically the Romans, who, in AD 70, destroyed Jerusalem and the Temple.

Phase Three There is a break between the second and third periods. Several events transpire after the 69th week, not during the 70th week: 1) Messiah shall be cut off. 2) Jerusalem shall be destroyed. That represents a 40-year gap. There is not only a 40-year gap; there is a bigger gap. We know that because the events of Daniel 9:27 have not yet been fulfilled. In fact, the entire church age spans the 69th and 70th weeks.

What will happen during this last week? Daniel 9:27 indicates that two things will happen. First, "he shall confirm a covenant with many for one week" (Dan. 9:27a). "He" refers to "the prince that shall come," a reference to the Antichrist. The Antichrist will make a treaty with Israel at the beginning of this seven-year period.

Second, "In the middle of the week, He shall bring an end to sacrifice and offering. And on the wing of abominations shall be one who makes desolate, Even until the consummation, which is determined, is poured out on the desolate" (Dan 9:27b). In the middle of these seven years, that is, after three and a half years, the Antichrist will break the covenant. He will cause all bloody and non-bloody sacrifices to cease. The fulfillment of this prophecy necessitates the reinstitution of the Mosaic sacrificial system in a Temple in Jerusalem.

This is called "the overspreading of abomination" that shall make desolate. Daniel 11:31 says Antiochus shall do it. Matthew 24:15 states that the Antichrist will do it. What Antiochus did is an illustration of what the Antichrist will do. What did Antiochus do?

In 1 Maccabees 1:45-54, the nature of the abomination in Antiochus's day is described. It states what Antiochus did. Following his order forbidding "burnt-offerings, and sacrifice, and drink-offerings in the Temple," he "set up the abomination of desolation upon the altar" and built "idol altars throughout the cities of Judah on every side." Then, 2 Maccabees 6:2 indicates that in this way, he polluted "the Temple in Jerusalem" and called it "the temple of Jupiter Olympus." It is unclear whether it was a statue of Jupiter Olympus (Zeus) or only a substitute altar used to worship him.

The Antichrist, like Antiochus, will set up in the holy place (the restored Temple) something detestable, like a false altar or a great statue, which will cause a desolate condition there.

The Riddle of Revelation

Jewish expositors have given this explanation of the 70th week of Daniel. Showers says, "*The Babylonian Talmud* states, 'Our Rabbis taught: In the seven-year cycle at the end of which the son of David will come.... at the conclusion of the septennate, the son of David will come'" (*Sanhedrin*, 97a, p. 654). (The word "septennate" refers to a period of seven years.)

Raphael Patai, writing about the messianic texts of Judaism, said, "The idea became entrenched that the coming of the Messiah will be preceded by greatly increased suffering.... This will last for seven years. And then, unexpectedly, the Messiah will come" (*The Messiah Texts*, pp. 95-96).

According to *The Babylonian Talmud*, "The advent of the Messiah was pictured as being preceded by years of great distress" (*Shabbath*, 118a, n. on "travails of the Messiah," p. 590).

The Dead Sea Scrolls and ancient rabbinic literature refer to the severe troubles of these seven years as "the birth pangs of the Messiah" (Burrows, "More Light on the Dead Sea Scrolls," in *Burrows on the Dead Sea Scrolls*, pp. 343-344). According to The Babylonian Talmud, the reason for this designation is that travail precedes birth, and this travail "precedes the birth of a new era—he messianic age" (*Sanhedrin*, 98b, n. on "birth pangs of the Messiah" p. 665). Just as a woman must go through a period of labor pains before her child is born into the world, so the world must go through seven years of labor pains before the messianic age is born into the world.

According to the *Apocalypse of Abraham* (ed. G. H. Box, p. 82), the birth pangs of the Messiah will involve such things as

The Tribulation

the sword (war), famine, pestilence, and wild beasts (the kinds of things involved in the beginning of birth pangs of Matthew 24:4-8 or the first four seals of Revelation 6:1-8). In addition, according to ancient Judaism, heaven will be the source of famine, pestilence, and earthquakes (Patai, *The Messiah Texts*, pp. 95-96, as cited in Renald E. Showers, *The Pre-Wrath Rapture View*, p. 14).

To sum up, God has a program for Israel to put an end to sin and establish a righteous kingdom, but before He does that, Israel will return, the Messiah will be cut off, and the Antichrist will make and break a covenant with Israel. Israel did return. Messiah did come. Jerusalem was destroyed, but there has not been a covenant or broken covenant (yet)!

The 70th week of Daniel 9 is often called the Tribulation. Technically, the Scripture has not used the word "tribulation" for these seven years, but it is a fitting title. The "time of Jacob's trouble" is called "great" (Jer. 30:7). This is a reference to the last half of the 70th week of Daniel (Showers, 2001, p. 16). The Hebrew word translated "trouble" means "writhing, anguish" (BDB, p. 297), "tightness, trouble, affliction, distress, tribulation" (Strong's *Hebrew Dictionary*). Therefore, the second half of the 70th week of Daniel is called "the Great Tribulation." Jesus calls the second half of the 70th week of Daniel the "Great Tribulation" (Mt. 24:15-21). Therefore, if the second half of the 70th week of Daniel is the "Great Tribulation," it is appropriate to designate the first half as the "Tribulation." In his book, *The Pre-Wrath Rapture View*, an interpretation he does not accept, Showers argues that it is appropriate to refer to the 70th week of Daniel as the Tribulation

(Showers, *The Pre-Wrath Rapture View*, pp. 12-17). He points out that we use words not found in the Bible for concepts such as "trinity," "incarnation," and "rapture."

Matthew 24

The Tribulation When the disciples asked Jesus, "When will these things be? And what *will be* the sign of Your coming, and of the end of the age?" (Mt. 24:3), He spoke of a false Christ (Mt. 24:4-5), war (Mt. 24:6-7a), famines (Mt. 24:7b), pestilences, and earthquakes (Mt. 24:7c), calling these the "**beginning** of sorrows" (Mt. 24:8). He went on to talk about persecution (Mt. 24:9-13), and the worldwide preaching of the gospel (Mt. 24:14). Then, He said, "The **end** will come" (Mt. 24:14). Clearly, He is describing a period with a beginning (Mt. 24:8) and an end (Mt. 24:14).

After describing a period that has a beginning and an end, Jesus says, "Therefore when **you see** the 'abomination of desolation,' spoken of by Daniel the prophet, standing in the holy place" (whoever reads, let him understand), then let those who are in Judea flee to the mountains" (Mt. 24:15-16). According to Daniel 9:27, the abomination of desolation occurs in the middle of a seven-year period, which, as we have seen, is called "the Tribulation." Therefore, the period Jesus describes in Mathew 24:4-14, a period with a beginning and an end, is the seven-year Tribulation. Like Daniel, Jesus divides it into two parts (Mt. 24:8, 14, 15). In other words, *the* sign (singular; see Mt. 24:3) of Christ's coming is the abomination of desolation.

The Tribulation

The Great Tribulation Also, since the abomination of desolation is the middle of the Tribulation (Dan. 9:27), what Jesus says in Matthew 24:15-28 is the second half of the Tribulation. Jesus calls this "the Great Tribulation" (Mt. 24:21). Jesus goes on to say that when the abomination of desolation occurs, Israel should flee into the wilderness (Mt. 24:16-20) because "there will be great tribulation, such as has not been since the beginning of the world until this time, no, nor ever shall be" (Mt. 24:21).

Second Coming After issuing warnings (Mt. 24:22-28), He says, "Immediately after the Tribulation of those days the sun will be darkened, and the moon will not give its light; the stars will fall from heaven, and the powers of the heavens will be shaken. Then the sign of the Son of Man will appear in heaven, and then all the tribes of the earth will mourn, and they will see the Son of Man coming on the clouds of heaven with power and great glory" (Mt. 24:29-30). According to Jesus, immediately after the Tribulation, there will be cosmic disturbances and the Son of Man will appear with power and great glory.

The coming of Christ in Matthew 24:30 refers to the Second Coming, not the Rapture. That is evident because He comes with power and great glory. He comes "with power" at the Second Coming for the Battle of Armageddon (Rev. 19:11, 15, 19, 21). He comes with "great glory" to establish the kingdom. In the context of the Olivet Discourse, Jesus discusses several other things, including a series of parables, before returning to the subject of His coming in chapter 25. In Matthew 25:31, Jesus says, "When the Son of Man comes in His glory and all His holy angels with

Him, then He will sit on the throne of His glory." Notice that when Jesus comes in His glory (Mt. 24:30), He will sit on the throne of His glory (Mt. 24:31), meaning He will establish the kingdom.

Some claim Matthew 24:30 refers to the coming of Christ at the Rapture, and Matthew 24:31 is the Rapture itself. It says, "And He will send His angels with a great sound of a trumpet, and they will gather together His elect from the four winds, from one end of heaven to the other." They contend that since Rapture in 1 Thessalonians 4 speaks of the same things: 1) Jesus, 2) believers, 3) angels, 4) trumpets, and 5) clouds, they are both describing the same event, namely the Rapture.

Granted, there are some similarities between Matthew 24 and 1 Thessalonians 4, but there are also differences. Similarities do not prove sameness. Differences demonstrate that similarities are not conclusive proof of sameness. The differences indicate that two different events are being described.

In Matthew, the Son of Man *comes on* the clouds; in 1 Thessalonians, believers are *in them*. In Matthew, the *angels* gather the elect; in 1 Thessalonians, the archangel, who is not mentioned in Matthew 24, speaks (see the voice of the archangel); he does not take any action. In Matthew, *there is no mention of* a resurrection; in 1 Thessalonians, the resurrection is the *central point*. In Matthew, the elect (Jews; see the next paragraph) are gathered *after* Christ's arrival to earth; in 1 Thessalonians, believers are gathered *in the air* (the implication in Jn. 14:1-3 is that they are then taken to heaven). This last comparison alone

The Tribulation

is sufficient to demonstrate that two entirely different events are being described.

Matthew 24 mentions the elect; 1 Thessalonians 4 does not. Who are the elect in Matthew 24:31? In Isaiah 65:7-16, there is a sharp contrast between the believing Jewish remnant and the unbelieving Israelites. God calls the believing remnant "mine elect" (Isa. 65:9). In the future, the elect remnant of Jews will be greatly blessed on the earth (Isa. 65:17-25; see also Isa. 11:5, 6, 12; Micah 2:12; Ezek. 36:24; 27:21). In Matthew 24, Jesus is speaking about the Jews, which is evident by His references to such things as the holy place (Mt. 24:15), the Sabbath (Mt. 24:20), and the Messiah (Mt 24:23-24) during the Tribulation (Mt. 24:29). In that context, Jesus uses the word "elect" three times (Mt. 24:22, 24, 31). In other words, the elect in Matthew 24:31 refers to believing Jews during the Tribulation.

Matthew 24 says angels will "gather together His elect from the four winds, from one end of heaven to the other." Jesus is using the language of Deuteronomy 30:4-5, which says, "If any of you are driven out to the farthest parts under heaven, from there the Lord will gather you and from there He will bring you. And the Lord your God will bring you to the land which your fathers possessed and you shall possess it." In other words, Jesus is talking about the regathering of Israel after His Second Coming.

Arnold Fruchtenbaum says, "The Matthew passage is a rather simple summary of all that the prophets had to say about the second facet of Israel's final restoration. Its purpose was to make clear that the worldwide regathering predicted by the prophets will be fulfilled only after the second coming" (Fruchtenbaum, cited by Ice).

Showers points out how this is a description of the regathering of Israel rather than the Rapture. "First, because of Israel's persistent rebellion against God, He declared that He would scatter the Jews 'into all the winds' (Ezek. 5:10, 12) or 'toward all winds' (Ezek. 17:21). In Zechariah 2:6, God stated that He did scatter them abroad 'as four winds of the heavens.' ... God did scatter the Jews all over the world. Next, God also declared that in the future, Israel would be gathered from the east, west, north, and south, 'from the ends of the earth' (Isa. 43:5-7). We should note that in the context of this promise, God called Israel His 'chosen' (vv. 10, 20).... Just as Jesus indicated that the gathering of His elect from the four directions of the world will take place in conjunction with 'a great trumpet' (literal translation of the Greek text of Mt. 24:21), so Isaiah 27:13 teaches that the scattered children of Israel will be gathered to their homeland in conjunction with the blowing of 'a great trumpet' (literal translation of the Hebrew). Gerhard Friedrich wrote that in that future eschatological day, 'a great horn shall be blown (Is. 27:13)' and the exiled will be brought back by that signal. Again, he asserted that in conjunction with the blowing of the great trumpet of Isaiah 27:13, 'There follows the gathering of Israel and the return of the dispersed to Zion.' It is significant to note that Isaiah 27:13, which foretells this future regathering of Israel, is the only specific reference in the Old Testament to a 'great' trumpet. Although Isaiah 11:11-12 does not refer to a great trumpet, it is parallel to Isaiah 27:13 because it refers to the

The Tribulation

same regathering of Israel. In its context, this passage indicates that when the Messiah (a root of Jesse, vv. 1, 10) comes to rule and transform the world as an 'ensign' (a banner), He will gather together the scattered remnant of His people Israel 'from the four corners of the earth' (Showers, cited by Ice).

To summarize, Matthew 24:31 refers to the regathering of Israel after the Second Coming of Christ, and 1 Thessalonians 4 describes the Rapture of the church. According to Matthew 24:31, angels will *gather* the elect (Israel) together. According to 1 Thessalonians, the Rapture is the simultaneous resurrection of the dead saints and the *catching up* of living saints together with them in the clouds to meet the Lord in the air (1 Thess. 4:15-17). Jesus will receive them *to Himself* (Jn. 14:3).

The cleansing of the Temple illustrates that similarity does not determine sameness. John 2:12-16 describes the Temple, oxen, sheep, and doves, as well as Jesus overturning the tables. Matthew 21:12-13 also discusses the Temple, the overturning of tables, and the selling of doves (see also Mark 11:15-17 and Luke 19:45-48). Some conclude that since the Gospel of John and the synoptic Gospels speak of the same things: 1) Jesus, 2) Temple, 3) selling doves, 4) overturning the tables, and 5) Jesus speaking, they are describing the same event. Granted, there are some similarities between the Gospel of John and the synoptic Gospels' account of the cleansing of the Temple, but there are also differences. John places the cleansing of the Temple *at the beginning* of Jesus' ministry. He says the first miracle was turning water into wine at Cana, and "after this," Jesus went to Capernaum, where He stayed "a few days." Then he says that since the Passover was at hand, Jesus went to Jerusalem, where He cleansed the Temple (John 2:11-14). The synoptic Gospels place the cleansing of the Temple in the week before the crucifixion. Aside from the nearly three-year gap, there are notable differences between the two events. In the first cleansing, Temple officials confronted Jesus immediately (Jn. 2:18), whereas in the second cleansing, the chief priests and scribes confronted Him the following day (Mt. 21:17-23). In the first event, Jesus made a whip of cords to drive out the sellers, but there is no mention of a whip in the second cleansing. Therefore, Jesus cleansed the Temple twice.

Similarities do not prove sameness. Differences demonstrate that similarities are not conclusive proof of sameness. The differences indicate that two different events are being described.

To sum up, Jesus gives the characteristics of the Tribulation from beginning to end (Mt. 24:4-14), refers to the middle of the Tribulation (Mt. 24:15) and describes some of the characteristics of the second half of the Tribulation, which He calls the "Great Tribulation" (Mt. 24:21). He then teaches that immediately after the Tribulation He will returned to set up His Kingdom.

1. False Christ (Mt. 24:4-5)
2. War (Mt. 24:6-7a)
3. Famines (Mt. 24:7b)
4. Pestilences and earthquakes (Mt. 24:7c)
5. Martyrdom (Mt. 24:9-13)
6. The middle of the Tribulation begins the Great Tribulation (Mt. 24:15-28)

The Tribulation

7. Cosmic disturbances come before His Second Coming (Mt. 24:29)
8. Christ returns to set up His kingdom (Mt. 24:30, 25:31).

Summary: Daniel 9 and Matthew 24 describe a period before the Second Coming of Christ to the establishment of the kingdom that Daniel says will last for seven years. It is commonly called the Tribulation.

Chapter 4

AN OVERVIEW OF REVELATION

An overview of any book of the Bible should consist of at least three things: the subject, the development of the subject, and the purpose.

The Subject of Revelation

"The Revelation of Jesus Christ, which God gave Him" (1:1a). The expression "The Revelation of Jesus Christ" can mean a "revelation about Christ" or a "revelation from Christ." The addition of the phrase "which God gave Him" indicates that the latter is the case, but that does not exclude the former. This revelation of Jesus Christ was given to him by God the Father, but the content of the book also indicates that this is a Revelation about Jesus Christ.

God gave this revelation to Christ for Him "to show His servants things which must shortly take place" (1:1b). The Greek word translated "shortly" means "speed, swiftness" (Abbott-Smith, p. 441; Arndt and Gingrich, p. 807). When used as an adverb, it can mean "quickly, at a rapid rate" or "quickly," meaning "in a short time, soon" (Arndt and Gingrich, who say that it is not always possible to make a clear distinction). Because the events of Revelation did not take place "soon" after the book was written, the word "shortly" in Revelation 1:1 (and in 22:6) must mean "at a rapid rate." When the time comes, these things will happen rapidly.

A different form of this word is translated "quickly" seven times in Revelation (2:5, 16; 3:11; 11:14; 22:7; 12, 20). There is an emphasis in Revelation on immanency (1:3; 3:3; 22:20). John says, "for the time is near" (1:3). The Greek word rendered "time" denotes not merely a point in time but a "season," a fixed and definite period, as in the expression "the time of harvest" (Smith). This period is described as "near," a Greek word used elsewhere in the New Testament to refer to prophetic events (Phil. 4:5). It simply indicates that the time is imminent but not necessarily soon. It could happen at any minute. It may be soon, but it may not be. As Barclay says, the early church lived in the expectation "of the coming of Christ at any moment."

Although the expression in the first verse, "the Revelation of Jesus Christ," means a revelation from Christ, what follows indicates that it is also about Christ. The outline of the book is given in verse 19: "Write the things which you have seen, and the things which are, and the things which will take place after this."

The first major part of the book is a vision. It is a vision of a man who is Jesus Christ. John said he saw "One like the Son of Man" (Rev. 1:12). The question is, "In what capacity is this a revelation of Jesus Christ?" For example, in Matthew, Jesus is

An Overview of Tribulation

revealed as the King of the Jews. In Mark, He is a servant. So, what is its function in the book of Revelation? One of the functions of the Son of Man is judge. Jesus says, "The Father judges no one, but has committed all judgment to the Son" (Jn. 5:22). Then, He adds that the Father "has given Him authority to execute judgment also, because He is the Son of Man" (Jn. 5:27).

In Revelation 5:2, a strong angel asked, "Who is worthy to open the scroll and loose its seal?" The answer is, "The Lion of the tribe of Judah" (Rev. 5:5). The title "Lion" refers to "Christ in His role as judge, rather than His role as Redeemer" (Van Kampen, *The Sign*, p. 182).

Thus, the book of Revelation is a revelation given to Jesus Christ, and at the same time, it reveals Him as the judge. It reveals Him as judge (1:9-20), first of the church (2:1-3:22), then of the world (4:1-19:21).

The Structure of Revelation

I. Prologue   1:1-8
II. Christ Revealed as Judge   1:9-20
III. Christ Revealed as Judge of the Church   2:1-3:22
     A. To Ephesus 2:1-7
     B. To Smyrna 2:8-11
     C. To Pergamos 2:12-17
     D. To Thyatira 2:18-29
     E. To Sardis 3:1-6

The Riddle of Revelation

    F. To Philadelphia 3:7-13
    G. To Laodicea 3:14-22
IV. Christ Revealed as Judge of the World   4:1-22:5
    A. The Seven Seal Judgments   4:1-8:2
        1. Prelude (in heaven)   4:1-5:14
        2. Six Seal Judgments   6:1-17
        3. Interlude   7:1-17
        4. Seventh Seal Judgment   8:1
    B. The Seven Trumpet Judgments   8:2-11:19
        1. Prelude (in heaven)   8:2-6
        2. Six Trumpet Judgments   8:7-9:21
        3. Interlude   10:1-11:14
        4. Seventh Trumpet Judgment   11:15-19
    C. The Explanatory Prophecies   12:1-14:20
    D. The Seven Bowl Judgments   15:1-16:21
        1. Prelude (in heaven)   15:1-8
        2. Seven Bowl Judgments   16:1-14
        3. Interlude   16:15
        4. Seven Bowl Judgments   16:16-21
    E. The Judgment of Babylon   17:1-18:24
    F. The Second Coming   19:1-21
    G. The Millennium   20:1-10
    H. The Great White Throne Judgment   20:11-15
V. The New Heavens and the New Earth   21:1-22:5
VI. Epilogue   22:6-20
VIII. Benediction   22:21

An Overview of Tribulation

There are three series of seven judgments: 1) seven seal judgments (4:1-8:2), seven trumpet judgments (8:3-11:19), and seven bowl judgments (15:1-16:21). That much is plain enough. The problem is the relationship between these judgments. Four common explanations of the relationship between the seals, trumpets, and judgments are: 1) The seals are in the first half. 2) The seals and the trumpets are in the first half. 3) The seals and the trumpets are in the last half. 4) The seals are in the first half, and the trumpets and bowls are in the second half. For an explanation of each of these, see Appendix I. The question is, "Are the seals, trumpets, and bowls judgments in successive order, or are they simultaneous?" Is there a strict chronological order, or is there recapitulation?

Succession The first impression is the three series of judgments are successive. The seventh seal *contains* the seven trumpet judgments (8:1-2), which seem to say that the trumpet judgments come after the seal judgments. In fact, the trumpet judgments are in response to events in the seal judgments (*cf.* 8:3-5 with 6:9-11). Furthermore, specific statements within the judgments indicate sequence. For example, "Do not harm the earth, the sea, or the trees till we have sealed the servants of our God on their foreheads" (7:3). The reference to five months (9:5) indicates progression.

There appears to be an increase in the intensity of the judgments. In the seal judgments, one-fourth of the earth is affected (6:8). Then, in the trumpet judgments, one-third of the earth is involved (8:7, 9, 10-12; 9:15). No percentage is given for any of the bowl judgments, but they follow the other judgments for they are "the seven *last* plagues and in them the wrath of God is *complete*" (15:1, italics added). Davis concludes, "Clearly, each series raises the crescendo of divine judgment to a higher pitch, and some form of sequence would best fit this framework" (Davis, p. 150).

Perhaps the strongest argument for some kind of sequence is the increase in intensity and the notation that the people did not repent (9:20-21; 16:9, 11, 21). Davis asks, "Does not the *gradual* rise in the intensity of the judgments bespeak a kind of divine reluctance to bring that last climactic stroke? Do we not sense something of the agonizing patience of God with profane men as He continues to offer grace in the midst of judgment and in wrath remembers mercy?" (Davis, p. 151, italics his).

Recapitulation Is the overall chronological order of the seals, trumpets, and bowls a *strict* chronological order, or is there also recapitulation within that overall scheme? An examination of the interludes in the seal and trumpet judgments indicates that there is a recapitulation within the basic chronological order.

There is a four-part pattern in the seal and trumpet judgments: 1) A prelude (a heavenly scene), 2) six of the seven judgments, 3) an interlude, and 4) the seventh judgment.

In the section on the seal judgments, after a prelude (4:1-5:14), John lists six seal judgments (6:1-17), pauses for an interlude (7:1-17), and then records the seventh seal judgment (8:1-2). He follows the same pattern in the trumpet judgments. After a prelude (8:3-6), he describes six trumpet judgments (8:7-9:21) and then pauses for another interlude (10:1-14). After that, he reveals the

An Overview of Tribulation

seventh trumpet judgment (11:15-19).

These intrudes do not chronologically *follow* the judgments they interrupt. Instead, the events of the interludes happen *during* the period of the series of judgments they interrupt. They recapitulate events that occurred during the time of those judgments. The interlude that interrupts the seal judgments takes place *during* the time of the six seal judgments. Likewise, the interlude in the trumpet judgments takes place *during* the time of the trumpet judgments.

For example, the interlude in the seal judgments describes something that happens *before* the sixth judgment. The interlude describes 144,000 "servants" (7:3). Their "service" begins before any harm comes to the earth, the sea, or the trees (7:3), which definitely indicates that it begins *before* the sixth seal judgment (6:12) and implies it takes place even before that (see the famine in 6:5-6), even possibly from the first seal judgment ("earth" in 7:3 and 6:4). If that is the case for the seal judgments, it is safe to assume it is also true for the trumpet judgments. The seal judgments set up the pattern. If so, the interlude in the trumpet judgments indicates that they cover 3½ years, during which time the two witnesses prophesy (11:3).

In other words, in the case of the seal and the trumpet judgments, John describes six judgments. Then, before recording the seventh judgment, he pauses to describe something not part of the judgments. These interludes describe something happening during the series of judgments that has nothing to do with judgments on earth, but rather what is happening with the saints.

The interlude between the sixth and seventh seal judgments describes 144,000 servants of God (7:1-8) and a great multitude of saints in heaven (7:9-17). The interlude between the sixth and seventh trumpet judgments describes a little book (10:1-11) and the ministry of the two witnesses (11:1-14). In short, after describing six judgments, John records an interlude, which is a flashback.

The recapitulation of the interludes proves that Revelation 6-11 is not in strict chronological order. That should not come as a surprise to anyone just reading the third division of Revelation. The seventh trumpet in Chapter 11 concludes with the ushering in of the kingdom, but the Millennium is not until chapter 20! Therefore, chapters 12-19 are a recapitulation. The third division of Revelation is not in *strict* chronological order.

Simultaneous To complicate matters, one element of the seal, trumpet, and bowl judgments seems to be simultaneous.

In the Olivet Discourse recorded in Matthew 24, Jesus said, "Immediately after the Tribulation of those days the sun will be darkened, and the moon will not give its light; the stars will fall from heaven, and the powers of the heavens will be shaken. Then the sign of the Son of Man will appear in heaven, and then all the tribes of the earth will mourn, and they will see the Son of Man coming on the clouds of heaven with power and great glory" (Mt. 24:29-30). Notice what happens immediately after the Tribulation and just before the Second Coming of Christ.

The sixth seal contains these words: "I looked when He opened the sixth seal, and behold, there was a great earthquake; and the

An Overview of Tribulation

sun became black as sackcloth of hair, and the moon became like blood. And the stars of heaven fell to the earth, as a fig tree drops its late figs when a mighty wind shakes it. Then the sky receded as a scroll when it is rolled up, and every mountain and island was moved out of its place" (Rev. 6:12-14).

A comparison between what Jesus said in Matthew 24 and the sixth seal judgment suggests that the sixth seal occurs immediately after the Tribulation and just before the Second Coming of Christ. In other words, the seal judgments *extend to* the Second Coming of Christ.

The seventh trumpet *extends to* the Second Coming. Just listen. "Then the seventh angel sounded: And there were loud voices in heaven, saying, 'The kingdoms of this world have become *the kingdoms* of our Lord and of His Christ, and He shall reign forever and ever!'" (11:15).

Likewise, the seventh bowl unquestionably *extends to* the end of the Tribulation: "Then the seventh angel poured out his bowl into the air, and a loud voice came out of the temple of heaven, from the throne, saying, 'It is done!'" (16:17). By the way, in the seventh bowl, we find, "Then every island fled away, and the mountains were not found" (16:20). It sounds like the seventh seal to me (6:14). Smith agrees. He points out that Revelation 6:14 states, "Every mountain and island was moved out of its place," and Revelation 16:20 inverts the order. However, the fact that it is the same event indicates that the time here is parallel to Revelation 6:14, namely, the close of the Tribulation (Smith).

Davis argues that the "*parallel phenomena* associated with the concluding member of each series may well imply that John intended them to be taken as parallel." Moreover, he points out that following the seventh seal, there are "noises, thunderings, lightnings, and an earthquake" (6:5), that the description of the seventh trumpet closes with "lightnings, noises, thunderings, an earthquake, and great hail" (11:19) and that the seventh bowl reveals similar manifestations, namely "noises and thunderings and lightnings; and there was a great earthquake, such a mighty and great earthquake as had not occurred since men were on the earth" (16:18) "And great hail from heaven fell upon men, *each hailstone* about the weight of a talent" (16:21; Davis, p. 152). Smith concurs, pointing out that at the end of the seals (6:5) and the end of the trumpets (11:9), there is a similar refrain, indicating that each series of judgments ends at the close of the Tribulation (Smith).

The sixth seal, the seventh trumpet, and the seventh bowl are not just describing something similar; they are covering the same event. Therefore, they must be simultaneous. Also, note that all three conclude with the Second Coming of Christ.

It might be objected that the sixth seal cannot be after the Tribulation because the seventh seal follows it. If the analysis of the content of the end of each series of judgments is correct (that they are parallel), it must be concluded that the *order of the visions* that reveal the judgments does not necessarily indicate the *order of the events* (Davis, p. 153).

An Overview of Tribulation

That is not to say that the *overall* structure of the three series is not chronological or that the events *within* the three series are not chronological. It is simply to acknowledge the obvious fact that the conclusion of each of the series is parallel. This is an inescapable conclusion for the trumpet and bowl judgments (they both state that they go all the way to the Second Coming) and when the sixth seal is compared to Matthew 24, it is apparent that it too is parallel with the other judgments at the Second Coming of Christ.

Granted, the similarity of events does not prove they are identical, but statements such as "every mountain and island was moved out of its place" in the sixth seal (6:14) and "every island fled away, and the mountains were not found" in the seventh bowl (16:20) are not just similar; they are the same event. How many times can every mountain be removed? The very nature of this event indicates it is the same event in both judgments.

Therefore, the seven seals, trumpets, and bowls run to the close of the end. "At the termination of each series, the note is unmistakably given, that such is the case" (Alford, vol. IV, p. 249). "Any system which does not recognize this common ending of the three seems to me to stand there by convicted of error" (Alford, vol. IV, p. 250).

If the seal, trumpet, and bowl judgments are basically sequential and yet each ends at the Second Coming, there must be gaps in the sequence. There must be a gap somewhere before the sixth seal judgment to allow for the first six trumpet judgments to occur because the sixth seal and the seventh trumpet are parallel to each other. Likewise, there must be a gap somewhere before the seventh trumpet to make room for the six bowl judgments for the seventh trumpet and the seventh bowl judgments to occur at the same time.

The conclusion is that although the three series of judgments are basically sequential, each extends to the Second Coming, and their ending is simultaneous or parallel with the others (Davis, p. 151). There is a sense in which there are sequence, recapitulation, and parallel aspects to the seal, trumpet, and bowl judgments.

Assuming that the first seal is at the beginning of the Tribulation and the first trumpet is at the beginning of the Great Tribulation, the arrangement of the three series of judgments is as follows.

Seals 1 2 3 4	5th Seal	(gap)	6th Seal
	Trumpets 1-6 (gap)		7th Trumpet
		(Bowls 1-6)	7th Bowl

The Purpose of Revelation

One of the purposes of Revelation is to comfort persecuted Christians. The emperor Domitian demanded worship, which led to persecution. Some were suffering, even to death (1:9; 2:10, 13; 6:9; 20:4). It must have looked as if wicked men were in control and evil would prevail. John wrote to reassure believers that Christ will eventually deal with the nations, judge sin, establish His kingdom, and bring in everlasting righteousness.

An Overview of Tribulation

The other purpose is to challenge complacent Christians. Some Believers were lax and lukewarm. The Ephesians had lost their first love (2:4), Pergamos and Thyatira allowed things they ought not (2:15-20), the Laodiceans were lukewarm (3:16). John wanted to challenge them to steadfastness and perseverance, so he writes to remind them that the Lord is returning and He has His reward with Him (22:12).

Summary: There is a threefold overall structure of the book of Revelation, which is in chronological order (1:19), but the third division is not in chronological order (11:19 and 16:17). The three series of judgments—the seals, the trumpets, and the bowls—are basically in sequence; they are in chronological order, but the interludes recapitulate, probably to the beginning of the series they interrupt, and all three series end at the Second Coming of Christ.

Chapter 5

THE SEVEN SEALS

The Seven Seal Judgments	4:1-8:2
1. Prelude (in heaven)	4:1-5:14
2. Six Seal Judgments	6:1-17
3. Interlude	7:1-17
4. Seventh Seal Judgment	8:1

Prelude

The Throne "After these things I looked, and behold, a door standing open in heaven. And the first voice which I heard was like a trumpet speaking with me, saying, 'Come up here, and I will show you things which must take place after this. Immediately, I was in the Spirit. And behold, a throne set in heaven, and **One sat on the throne**. And He who sat there was like a jasper and a sardius stone in appearance; and there was a rainbow around the throne, in appearance like an emerald. Around the throne were twenty-four thrones, and on the thrones I saw twenty-four elders sitting, clothed in white robes; and they had crowns of gold on their heads. And from the throne proceeded lightnings, thunderings, and voices. Seven lamps of fire were burning before the throne, which are the seven Spirits of God" (4:1-5, bold type added). The occupant of the throne is not identified as a person. Later, it becomes apparent that the One who "sat on the throne (4:2) is the "Lord God Almighty" (4:8), that is God the Father. For elders, see 4:9 ff.

The Living Creatures "Before the throne, there was a sea of glass, like crystal. And in the midst of the throne, and around the throne, were **four living creatures** full of eyes in front and in back. The first living creature was like a lion, the second living creature like a calf, the third living creature had a face like a man, and the fourth living creature was like a flying eagle. The four living creatures, each having six wings, were full of eyes around and within. And they do not rest day or night, saying: "Holy, holy, holy, Lord God Almighty, who was and is and is to come!" (4:6-8, bold type added). The four living creatures are angels.

The Twenty-four Elders "Whenever the living creatures give glory and honor and thanks to Him who sits on the throne, who lives forever and ever, the **twenty-four elders** fall down before Him who sits on the throne and worship Him who lives forever and ever, and cast their crowns before the throne, saying: "You are worthy, O Lord, To receive glory and honor and power; for You created all things, and by Your will they exist and were created" (4:9-10, bold type added). The elders are clothed in white (4:4). Sardis was told that overcomers would be "clothed in white garments" (3:5) and that the church at Laodicea was counseled to buy "white garments" (3:18), and now the elders in heaven are clothed in white robes (the Greek word translated "robes" in 4:4 is the same one rendered "garments" in 3:5, 18). The elders wear

The Seven Seals

crowns of gold on their heads (4:4). Members of the church are told they will receive crowns. (2:10; 3:11, same Greek word). The elders are redeemed kings and priests (5:8-10). The elders represent the church. They are called elders because they represent a group, as did the elders at the Jerusalem Council in Acts 15 (Smith). Their crowns indicate they had been rewarded. That means they have appeared before the Judgment Seat of Christ, which is after the Rapture. Therefore, the Rapture is Pre-tribulational.

The Scroll "And I saw in the right hand of Him who sat on the throne a scroll written inside and on the back, sealed with seven seals" (5:1). These seals were fixed on the edge of the scroll so that each seal had to be broken successively if the scroll was to be unrolled (Walvoord; Morris).

The Strong Angel "Then I saw a strong angel proclaiming with a loud voice, 'Who is worthy to open the scroll and to loose its seals?' And no one in heaven or on the earth or under the earth was able to open the scroll, or to look at it. So I wept much, because no one was found worthy to open and read the scroll, or to look at it" (5:2-4). John had been promised that he would be shown things to come (4:1). It now appears that this promise will not be kept. John is disappointed

The Lion "But one of the elders said to me, "Do not weep. Behold, the Lion of the tribe of Judah, the Root of David, has prevailed to open the scroll and to loose its seven seals" (5:5). The expression "the Lion of the tribe of Judah" is taken from Genesis 49:9-10, where the future ruler is said to come from the tribe of Judah, "the lion tribe" (Walvoord).

The Riddle of Revelation

The Lamb John says, "And I looked, and behold, in the midst of the throne and of the four living creatures, and in the midst of the elders, stood a Lamb as though it had been slain, having seven horns and seven eyes, which are the seven Spirits of God sent out into all the earth. Then He came and took the scroll out of the right hand of Him who sat on the throne" (5:6-7). An elder told John to look at a Lion, but when John looked, he saw a Lamb. The Lion was a Lamb. When Jesus came the first time, He came as a lamb. When He returns, He will come as a lion. As the lamb, He is the Savior. As the Lion, He is the Judge.

The Song "Now when He had taken the scroll, the four living creatures and the twenty-four elders fell down before the Lamb, each having a harp, and golden bowls full of incense, which are the prayers of the saints. And they sang a new song, saying: 'You are worthy to take the scroll, and to open its seals; for You were slain, and have redeemed us to God by Your blood out of every tribe and tongue and people and nation, and have made us kings and priests to our God; And we shall reign on the earth'" (5:8-10). The English text makes it sound as if the four living creatures and the elder sing. In Greek, the living creatures are neuter and the elders are masculine and "each" is masculine. Therefore, what follows "each" in verse 8 through 10 is a reference to the elders.

The Lamb is worthy to open the scroll and break the seals because He was slain, because He has redeemed people from every nation on earth, and because He has made believers kings and priests. As priests, the church shall serve, and as kings, the church will reign (Mounce).

The elders are not angels because angels are not redeemed and do not receive crowns. Moreover, elders are a distinct group from angels (5:11). Also, the elders are representative, as twenty-four is not a sufficient number to come from "out of every tribe and tongue and people and nation" (Smith).

The Multitude "Then I looked, and I heard the voice of many angels around the throne, the living creatures, and the elders; and the number of them was ten thousand times ten thousand, and thousands of thousands, saying with a loud voice: 'Worthy is the Lamb who was slain to receive power and riches and wisdom, and strength and honor and glory and blessing!'" (5:11-12). The number indicates that a number beyond human calculation (Mounce). The angels shout rather than sing (Swete). They shout a sevenfold praise to the Lamb.

All Creatures "And every creature which is in heaven and on the earth and under the earth and such as are in the sea, and all that are in them, I heard saying: 'Blessing and honor and glory and power be to Him who sits on the throne, and to the Lamb, forever and ever!'" (5:13). This fourfold doxology repeats three elements of praise of the angels (5:12), but those retained are in a different order, and the Greek word for "power" is different.

Living Creatures "Then the four living creatures said, 'Amen!' And the twenty-four elders fell down and worshiped Him who lives forever and ever" (5:14). To the doxology of the "cosmic congregation" and the angels, the four living creatures say "Amen" (Smith).

Six Seals

The First Seal: The Antichrist "Now I saw when the Lamb opened one of the seals; and I heard one of the four living creatures saying with a voice like thunder, 'Come and see.' And I looked, and behold, a white horse. He who sat on it had a bow; and a crown was given to him, and he went out conquering and to conquer" (6:1-2). Based on Jesus riding a white horse in Revelation 19, some says this is Jesus, but "the two riders have nothing in common beyond the white horse" (Swete). The rider in chapter 6 has a bow, while the One in chapter 19 has a sword, and the crowns are also different (Mounce). The crown in chapter 6 is a victor's crown, not a sovereign's crown. The rider is the Antichrist. At the beginning of the Tribulation, the Antichrist scores several peaceful victories, but he is bent on conquest.

The seals reveal instruments of God's wrath. The first seal is the coming of the Antichrist (Rev. 6:1-2). God has used Satan as an instrument of His wrath. "Again, the *anger* of the LORD was aroused against Israel, and He moved David against them to say, 'Go, number Israel and Judah'" (2 Sam. 24:1, italics added). "Now Satan stood up against Israel, and moved David to number Israel" (1 Chron. 21:1). Later, in the book of Revelation, the trumpet judgments include the release of demons (see 9:1-11, esp. the comments on verse 11 below). God uses demons to judge (see comments on 11:12-14).

The Second Seal: War "When He opened the second seal, I heard the second living creature saying, 'Come and see.' Another horse, fiery red, went out. And it was granted to the one who sat on it to take peace from the earth, and that people should kill one another; and there was given to him a great sword" (6:3-4). The great sword is a "symbol of bloodshed" (Swete). The rider "exchanges the empty bow for a sword" (Wiersbe). This rider takes peace from the earth.

The second seal is war (Rev. 6:3-4). God has used war as an instrument of His wrath. In describing the war that the Lord will send against Babylon (Jer. 50:9), Jeremiah says, "Because of the wrath of the LORD, she [Babylon] shall not be inhabited, but she shall be wholly desolate. Everyone who goes by Babylon shall be horrified and hiss at all her plagues" (Jer. 50:13).

The Third Seal: Famine "When He opened the third seal, I heard the third living creature say, 'Come and see.' So I looked, and behold, a black horse, and he who sat on it had a pair of scales in his hand. And I heard a voice in the midst of the four living creatures saying, 'A quart of wheat for a denarius, and three quarts of barley for a denarius; and do not harm the oil and the wine'" (6:5-6). The voice in the midst of the four living creatures must be a divine voice, as it originates from among them (Morris). Everything about this seal speaks of famine. In the Old Testament, "to eat bread by weight" indicates great scarcity (Lev. 26:26; Ez. 4:16). The famine causes enormous inflation.

The third seal is famine, which causes inflation (Rev. 6:5-6). God has used famine as an instrument of His wrath. "Take heed to yourselves, lest your hearts be deceived, and you turn aside and serve other gods and worship them, lest the Lord's anger be aroused against you and He showed up to the heavens so that there be no rain, and the land yield no produce, and you perish quickly from the good land which the Lord is giving you" (Deut. 11:16-17).

The Fourth Seal: Death "When He opened the fourth seal, I heard the voice of the fourth living creature saying, 'Come and see.' So I looked, and behold, a pale horse. And the name of him who sat on it was Death, and Hades followed with him. And power was given to them over a fourth of the earth, to kill with sword, with hunger, with death, and by the beasts of the earth" (6:7-8). Christ has the keys to death and Hades (1:18). God is sovereign. Death and Hades only exercise power as they are allowed (Morris).

The fourth seal is death (Rev. 6:3-4). Famine, death, and pestilence are spoken of in the Old Testament as God's wrath and the Day of the Lord. In Ezekiel 7, God repeatedly refers to His judgment as His anger (see "I will send My anger against you in verse 3, "Now upon you I will soon pour out My fury, and spend My anger upon you" in verse 8, and "My wrath *is* on all their multitude" in verse 14) and explains this judgment includes the sword, pestilence, and famine" (verse 15). Then, this is called "the day of the wrath of the LORD" (verse 19).

In the New Testament, God uses human government as an instrument of His wrath. Romans 13:4 says, "For it is a minister of God to you for good. But if you do what is evil, be afraid; for it does not bear the sword for nothing; for it is a minister of God, an avenger who brings wrath on the one who practices evil."

The Seven Seals

In a footnote, Van Kampen says that many Old Testament passages depict God's wrath being expressed through war, famine, wild animals, or plagues "(e.g., Lev. 26:21-28; Num. 11:33; 16:46; 25:8-11; Deut. 11:17; 32:22-25; 2 Chron. 29:8-9; 36:16, 17; Isa. 19:12; Jer. 14:12; 15:1-9; 16:4, 10, 11; 19:7-9, 15; 21:5-7; 24:10; 48:8, 11-13; Ezek. 4:16, 17; 5:11-17; 6:3, 11, 12; 7:3, 8, 14, 19; 18:8; 21:19; 33:19-22; 38:19-22; 39:4)" (Van Kampen, p. 479, fn. 3).

Conclusion: The four seal judgments of the wrath of God. Since the church is delivered from the wrath of God (1 Thess. 5:9), the Rapture is Pre-tribulational.

Many have pointed out the parallel between the first four signs in Matthew 24 (false Christ, war, famine, and death caused by pestilence and earthquakes) and the first four seals in Revelation 6 (Antichrist, war, famine, and death). Jesus calls the first four signs "the beginning of sorrows" (Mt. 24:8), a reference to the first half of the Tribulation (Mt. 24:14, 15, 21). If the first four signs in Matthew 24 are in the first half of the Tribulation and are parallel to the first four seals, the first four seals are in the first half of the Tribulation.

Characteristic	Matthew 24	Revelation 6
	Beginning of Sorrows	Four Horsemen
False Christ	Matthew 24:4-5	Revelation 6:1-2
War	Matthew 24:6-7a	Revelation 6:3-4
Famine	Matthew 24:7b	Revelation 6:5-6
Death	Matthew 24:7c	Revelation 6:7-8

The Fifth Seal: Martyrdom "When He opened the fifth seal, I saw under the altar the souls of those who had been slain for the word of God and for the testimony which they held. And they cried with a loud voice, saying, 'How long, O Lord, holy and true, until You judge and avenge our blood on those who dwell on the earth?' then a white robe was given to each of them; and it was said to them that they should rest a little while longer, until both the number of their fellow servants and their brethren, who would be killed as they were, was completed" (6:9-11). They are said to be *under* the altar because the blood of the sacrifices was poured out under the altar (Ex. 29:12; Lev. 4:7). The martyr's plea for "vindication" (Mounce; Wiersbe). In response to their plea (6:10), the martyrs are given white robes and told that martyrdom would continue for a short time. The white robes are the righteousness of the saints (19:8).

Note the fifth sign in Matthew 24 is martyrdom (Mt. 24:9), and the fifth seal in Revelation 6 is also related to martyrdom (6:9-11). These martyrs are in the "Great Tribulation" (7:14). Does this not indicate that the first four seals in Revelation 6 are in the first half of the Tribulation ("the beginning of sorrows") and the fifth seal is in the second half of the Tribulation? Is that why the first four seals are marked off by four horsemen (6:1-8)?

The middle of the Tribulation is between the fourth and fifth seal judgments. It is in the middle of the Tribulation, when the Antichrist breaks the covenant and persecution and martyrdom begin.

The Sixth Seal: Cosmic Disturbances "I looked when He opened the sixth seal, and behold, there was a great earthquake; and the sun became black as sackcloth of hair, and the moon became like blood. And the stars of heaven fell to the earth, as a fig tree drops its late figs when it is shaken by a mighty wind. Then the sky receded as a scroll when it is rolled up, and every mountain and island was moved out of its place" (6:12-14). Note that the sixth seal includes the sun becoming black, the moon becoming like blood, and the stars of heaven falling to the earth. Matthew 24:29 says, "Immediately after the tribulation of those days the sun will be darkened, and the moon will not give its light; the stars will fall from heaven, and the powers of the heavens will be shaken." In other words, the sixth seal and Matthew 24:29 are describing the same thing. These descriptions are in the form of a simile (Mounce).

Revelation 6:12-14 describes the end of the Tribulation. Verse 14 says, "Every mountain and island was moved out of its place." The sixth seal looks to the troubles which "precede the end" (Swete), "cosmic disturbances which are to herald the last days begin" (Mounce). Likewise, the seventh bowl unquestionably *extends to* the end of the Tribulation: "Then the seventh angel poured out his bowl into the air, and a loud voice came out of the temple of heaven, from the throne, saying, 'It is done!'" (16:17). "Then every island fled away, and the mountains were not found" (16:20). In other words every mountain being moved is at the end of the Tribulation. Smith agrees. He points out that Revelation 6:14 states, "Every mountain and island was moved out of its place," and Revelation 16:20 inverts the order. However, the fact that it is the same event indicates that the time here is parallel to Revelation 6:14, namely, the close of the Tribulation (Smith).

"And the kings of the earth, the great men, the rich men, the commanders, the mighty men, every slave and every free man, hid themselves in the caves and in the rocks of the mountains, and said to the mountains and rocks, 'Fall on us and hide us from the face of Him who sits on the throne and from the wrath of the Lamb! For the great day of His wrath has come, and who is able to stand?'"(6:15-17). All classes of society will be "terror-struck by the sign of the approaching end" (Swete). The text states that the wrath "has come," indicating it has already occurred, not that it is about to happen.

The *context* of Revelation 6:17 suggests that "has come" is in the past, not the future. The word "come" ties the first four seal judgments to the wrath in verse 17, which means the wrath in Revelation 6:17 is linked to the first seal. When each of the first four seals is open, one of the living creatures says, "Come and see" (6:1, 3, 5, 7). Then, in *response* to the four seal judgments, martyrs ask how much longer it will be before God judges those who dwell on the earth (Rev. 6:9-11). In *response* to the first four seals, the unsaved say the great Day of God's wrath has come. The structure of the chapter indicates that there are four seal judgments, followed by the responses of the martyrs, and then the responses of the unbelievers. In response to the four seal judgments, the unbelievers say God's wrath has come.

The *grammar* of Revelation 6:17 suggests that "has come" is in the past, not the future. The Greek word translated "has come" is an aorist indicative. Greek grammarians Dana and Mantey explain, "It [aorist] has no essential temporal significance, its time

The Seven Seals

relations being found only in the indicative, where it is used as past (Dana and Mantey, p. 193).

Ryrie points out that the Pre-wrath Rapture view says that the verb tense in Revelation 6:17 may mean "it is about to come," but "this is not how John uses it in other places in Revelation. In 11:18; 14:7, 15; 18:10, and 19:7, the same verb in the same tense as in 6:17 is used of events and people that are present and already on the scene, not that are about to come in the (howsoever near) future" (Ryrie, *Rapture*, pp. 94-95). All of Ryrie's examples are aorist indicative.

Before leaving the discussion of the seals, note the parallel between Matthew 24:4-31 and Revelation 6:1-17. The items listed and the order in which they are given are false Christ (Mt. 24:4-5; Rev. 6:1-2), war (Mt. 24:6-7a; Rev. 6:3-4), famine (Mt. 24:7b; Rev. 6:5-6), death (Mt. 24:7c; Rev. 6:7-8), martyrdom (Mt. 24:9; Rev. 6:9-11), and cosmic disturbances (6:12-17). Since what is being described in Matthew 24 is the Tribulation (Mt. 24:21) just before the Second Coming (Mt. 24:29-30), the parallel between Matthew 24 and Revelation 6 proves that the seal judgments are in the Tribulation.

The four horsemen in Revelation 6 cover the first half of the Tribulation. So do "the beginning of sorrows" in Matthew 24, therefore, the fifth seal is after the middle of the Tribulation. The sixth seal is at the end of the Tribulation, just before the Second Coming (*cf.* Mt. 24:29-30 with Rev. 6:12-14. The cosmic disturbances are just before the Second Coming.

Interlude

Sealed Servants "After these things I saw four angels standing at the four corners of the earth, holding the four winds of the earth, that the wind should not blow on the earth, on the sea, or on any tree. Then I saw another angel ascending from the east, having the seal of the living God. And he cried with a loud voice to the four angels to whom it was granted to harm the earth and the sea, saying, "Do not harm the earth, the sea, or the trees till we have sealed the servants of our God on their foreheads" (7:1-3). This probably occurs before the seal judgment. They have "His [the Lamb's] Father's name written on their foreheads" (14:1).

"And I heard the number of those who were sealed. One hundred and forty-four thousand of all the tribes of the children of Israel were sealed: of the tribe of Judah twelve thousand were sealed; of the tribe of Reuben twelve thousand were sealed; of the tribe of Gad twelve thousand were sealed; of the tribe of Asher twelve thousand were sealed; of the tribe of Naphtali twelve thousand were sealed; of the tribe of Manasseh twelve thousand were sealed; of the tribe of Simeon twelve thousand were sealed; of the tribe of Levi twelve thousand were sealed; of the tribe of Issachar twelve thousand were sealed; of the tribe of Zebulun twelve thousand were sealed; of the tribe of Joseph twelve thousand were sealed; of the tribe of Benjamin twelve thousand were sealed" (7:4-8). These 144,000 Jewish converts are the first fruits (14:4), suggesting they were saved at the beginning of the Tribulation.

The Seven Seals

Serving Saints "After these things I looked, and behold, a great multitude which no one could number, of all nations, tribes, peoples, and tongues, standing before the throne and before the Lamb, clothed with white robes, with palm branches in their hands and crying out with a loud voice, saying, "Salvation belongs to our God who sits on the throne, and to the Lamb!" (7:9-10). The phrase "after these things" denotes "merely a subsequent (Smith). The great multitude are saints in heaven, thanking God for their salvation.

"All the angels stood around the throne and the elders and the four living creatures, and fell on their faces before the throne and worshiped God, saying: 'Amen! Blessing and glory and wisdom, thanksgiving and honor and power and might, be to our God forever and ever. Amen'" (7:11-12). This is a sevenfold doxology of praise to God for the multitude who have been saved and delivered.

"Then one of the elders answered, saying to me, 'Who are these arrayed in white robes, and where did they come from?' And I said to him, 'Sir, you know.' So he said to me, 'These are the ones who come out of the great tribulation, and washed their robes and made them white in the blood of the Lamb'" (7:13-14). The great multitude are saints who were martyred. The elders and the great multitude indicate two groups of redeemed in heaven during the Tribulation (Smith).

"Therefore, they are before the throne of God, and serve Him day and night in His temple. And He who sits on the throne will dwell among them. They shall neither hunger anymore nor thirst anymore; the sun shall not strike them, nor any heat; "for the Lamb who is in the midst of the throne will shepherd them and lead them to living fountains of waters. And God will wipe away every tear from their eyes" (7:15-17). The great multitude who delivered hardships may be an oblique reference to the sufferings experienced during the Tribulation (Walvoord).

Since the first group is called servants, the implication is that they were the ones who led the great multitude to Christ. That is not explicitly stated, but it is a logical deduction (Wiersbe). In Revelation, the 144,000 are called the first fruits (14:4) and servants (7:3). The 144,000 are the servants of the Tribulation, who lead multitudes to Christ. In the Old Testament, the Jews preached the gospel to the Gentiles. In the New Testament, the Gentiles preached to the Jews. In the Tribulation, the Jews will again preach the gospel to the Gentiles.

Seventh Seal

"When He opened the seventh seal, there was silence in heaven for about half an hour. And I saw the seven angels who stand before God, and to them were given seven trumpets" (8:1-2). The silence is connected to the opening of the seventh seal, the trumpet judgments. The trumpet judgments are so ominous that the angels, elders, and martyrs were "simply awestruck at what they saw" (Wiersbe). For silence in the face of the Day of the Lord, see Zephaniah 1:7.

Chapter 6

THE SEVEN TRUMPETS

The Seven Trumpet Judgments	8:2-11:19
1. Prelude (in heaven)	8:2-6
2. Six Trumpet Judgments	8:7-9:21
3. Interlude	10:1-11:14
4. Seventh Trumpet Judgment	11:15-19

Prelude

"Then another angel, having a golden censer, came and stood at the altar. He was given much incense, that he should offer it with the prayers of all the saints upon the golden altar which was before the throne. And the smoke of the incense, with the prayers of the saints, ascended before God from the angel's hand. Then the angel took the censer, filled it with fire from the altar, and threw it to the earth. And there were noises, thunderings, lightnings, and an earthquake. So the seven angels who had the seven trumpets prepared themselves to sound" (8:2-6). This is a pictorial way of saying the prayers of the saints came before God (see 6:10). The very container that symbolizes the prayers of the saints becomes the container of judgment. In response to the prayers of the saints for God to avenge the wicked world, God pours out judgment on the world.

Six Trumpets

The First Trumpet "The first angel sounded: and hail and fire followed, mingled with blood, and they were thrown to the earth. And a third of the trees were burned up, and all green grass was burned up" (8:7). The first four trumpet judgments are united. They are all bound together by the fact that they share a common vision. "I saw" is not repeated until verse 13, when the last three trumpets are introduced by "woe" (Smith). Moreover, the first four trumpet judgments primarily affect "inanimate nature," although animals and humans are indirectly affected. Direct judgment on humans is not until the last three trumpet judgments. The division is four, two, one. The last is "singles out for emphasis by an interlude between the sixth and the seventh" (Morris).

Either hail and fire mingled with blood means blood is in the hail and fire, or the result is bloodshed (Walvoord). The fire could be a "severe electrical storm" (Wiersbe). The result is that a third of the trees and the grass are destroyed. This means the destruction of pasture lands, which would "devastate the meat and milk industries" (Wiersbe), an economic disaster.

The Second Trumpet "Then the second angel sounded: and something like a great mountain burning with fire was thrown into the sea and a third of the sea became blood. And a third of the living creatures in the sea died, and a third of the ships were destroyed" (8:8-9). The word "like" indicates that a figure of speech is involved. In other words, a large object fell from heaven (Walvoord). Perhaps the burning mountain was a meteor. The results are an ecological disaster.

The Third Trumpet "Then the third angel sounded: and a great star fell from heaven, burning like a torch and it fell on a third of the rivers and on the springs of water. The name of the star is Wormwood. A third of the waters became wormwood, and many men died from the water, because it was made bitter" (8:10-11). The expression "burning like a torch" indicates that some symbolism is involved. Walvoord says that a "reasonable literalness" is that the star is a heavenly body or a mass from outer space, burning as it enters the atmosphere. Falling from heaven indicates that God is "an active agent" in this event (Mounce). The result is the destruction of a third of the freshwater. The water became wormwood, meaning it became bitter as wormwood (Mounce).

The Fourth Trumpet "Then the fourth angel sounded: and a third of the sun was struck, a third of the moon, and a third of the stars, so that a third of them were darkened. A third of the day did not shine, and likewise the night" (8:12). A partial eclipse would produce partial darkness, but here a partial eclipse results in shortening of daylight and moonlight. The vision and interpretation are inconsistent, indicating that John emphasizes the partial nature of the eclipse (Swete).

"And I looked, and I heard an angel flying through the midst of heaven, saying with a loud voice 'Woe, woe, woe to the inhabitants of the earth, because of the remaining blasts of the trumpet of the three angels who are about to sound!" (8:13). Three more angels are yet to blow their trumpets (9:12; 11:14, the third maybe 12:12, Morris). The worst is yet to come.

The Fifth Trumpet: Demonic Locusts "Then the fifth angel sounded: And I saw a star fallen from heaven to the earth. To him was given the key to the bottomless pit. And he opened the bottomless pit, and smoke arose out of the pit like the smoke of a great furnace. So the sun and the air were darkened because of the smoke of the pit" (9:1-2). The fifth trumpet judgment, also known as the first woe (9:12), begins with a fallen star. The star in Revelation 8:8, 10 is a falling material mass. The star here is a symbol of a person, as subsequent statements indicate. The fallen star is Satan (9:11), although not everyone agrees (Morris provides a list of options). "The fallen star is *given* the key to the bottomless pit. He does not have the authority to open the pit; it has to be given to him. This is another way of emphasizing God's sovereignty (Morris).

The Greek word translated "bottomless" is used of the "abyss," the abode of demons (Lk. 8:31). In Revelation, it is the intermediate place for the fallen angels, the demons, the beast, the False Prophet, and Satan (9:1, 2, 11; 11:7; 20:1, 3). Their final place of punishment will be the lake of fire (20:10, 14, 15). When the bottomless pit is opened, it releases so much smoke that the air becomes polluted, the sky is darkened, and the sunlight is obscured. The point is that the amount of smoke is so great that even the light of the sun is blotted out (Morris).

"Then out of the smoke locusts came upon the earth. And to them was given power, as the scorpions of the earth have power. They were commanded not to harm the grass of the earth, or any green thing, or any tree, but only those men who do not have the seal of God on their foreheads. And they were not given authority to kill them, but to torment them for five months. Their torment was like the torment of a scorpion when it strikes a man" (9:3-5). The locusts belong to the family of the cricket and grasshopper. They breed in the desert and invade cultivated lands for food. They travel in immense numbers, four or five miles in breadth and ten or twelve miles in length, with a height so deep (as much as one hundred feet) that the sun cannot penetrate them.

The locusts from the pit are not natural locusts (Walvoord). Locusts devour herbage and strip trees, but these are forbidden to do that (9:4). They were permitted to torment for five months human beings who had not received the seal of God, a reference to the sealing of the 144,000 and "may extend as far as this plague is concerned to all; who know the Lord in that day" (Walvoord).

"In those days men will seek death and will not find it; they will desire to die, and death will flee from them" (9:6). Five months is a limited time (Mounce), but the torment lasts so long that people desire to die (Jer. 8:3). They could not, perhaps because "the sting caused physical incapacity" (Hodges, p. 89). Pointing out "flee" is in the present tense, one commentator says, "Death keeps running from them" (Morris). A Latin writer, Cornelius Gallus, says: "Worse than any wound is to wish to die and yet not be able to do so" (Gallus, cited by Barclay).

"The shape of the locusts was like horses prepared for battle. On their heads were crowns of something like gold, and their faces were like the faces of men. They had hair like women's hair, and their teeth were like lions' teeth. And they had breastplates like breastplates of iron, and the sound of their wings was like the sound of chariots with many horses running into battle. They had tails like scorpions, and there were stings in their tails. Their power was to hurt men for five months" (9:7-10). The point here is that these locusts were like horses *prepared for battle*. Furthermore, they had gold-looking crowns on their heads "like conquerors" and faces like humans, suggesting "intelligence" (Swete). The description of women's hair and Lion's teeth puts them "among the most bizarre creatures in the Apocalypse" (Mounce). The breastplate of iron implies they are "difficult to destroy" (Morris), "immune to destruction" (Walvoord). The reference to wings suggests speed (Walvoord).

"And they had as king over them the angel of the bottomless pit, whose name in Hebrew is Abaddon, but in Greek he has the name Apollyon" (9:11). Proverbs says, "The locusts have no king" (Prov. 30:27), but these unusual, unnatural locusts from the bottomless have a king. Satan is the king and angel of the bottomless pit (Smith; Walvoord), but not all agree (Mounce). The king's name is "Abaddon," a Hebrew word meaning "destruction" (Smith), and "Apollyon" is a Greek word meaning "destroyer." These locusts are unnatural. They are "possessed by demons" (Smith, p. 143). Thus, in addition to the natural plagues of the first four trumpet judgments, people are now afflicted by demons (Walvoord).

"One woe is past. Behold, still two more woes are coming after these things" (9:12). The e`nd is not yet. Only the first woe is past. The word "woe" in Scripture refers to "some great calamity, usually a judgment from God (Walvoord).

The Sixth Trumpet: Demonic Hordes "Then the sixth angel sounded: And I heard a voice from the four horns of the golden altar which is before God, saying to the sixth angel who had the trumpet, 'Release the four angels who are bound at the great river Euphrates'" (9:13-14). Smith says that the sixth trumpet judgment is "probably the greatest of all" the judgments before the coming of Christ, because of the great amount of detail given to it. He says that it extends through Revelation 11:14. The mention of the altar suggests, "This judgment like those preceding is partially an answer to the prayers of persecuted saints on earth" (Walvoord). There is nothing in the text "to prevent" the Euphrates River from being taken literally (Alford).

"So the four angels, who had been prepared for the hour and day and month and year, were released to kill a third of mankind" (9:15). The expression "the hour and day and month and year" indicates that the exact hour had been appointed by God (Walvoord). John has already said that 25% of the population has been killed (6:8). Now, an additional third is killed. Thus, after this judgment, 50% of the population of the earth is destroyed.

"Now the number of the army of the horsemen was two hundred million; I heard the number of them" (9:16). Apparently, the angels use a human army to accomplish the destruction of a third of humanity (see Morris). The literal interpretation is not impossible (Walvoord). If the number is literal, it would be the "largest armed force ever known to man" (Walvoord).

"And thus I saw the horses in the vision: those who sat on them had breastplates of fiery red, hyacinth blue, and sulfur yellow; and the heads of the horses were like the heads of lions; and out of their mouths came fire, smoke, and brimstone. By these three plagues a third of mankind was killed; by the fire and the smoke and the brimstone which came out of their mouths. For their power is in their mouth and in their tails; for their tails are like serpents, having heads; and with them they do harm" (9:17-19). The horses had lion-like heads and fire and brimstone came out of their mouths. Whether it is or not, the horses are literal; they are an awesome picture of destruction. The description indicates that they are "demon-possessed, hideous monstrosities" (Smith). Fire, smoke, and brimstone are three judgments (9:18) by which a third of mankind is killed.

"But the rest of mankind, who were not killed by these plagues, did not repent of the works of their hands, that they should not worship demons, and idols of gold, silver, brass, stone, and wood, which can neither see nor hear nor walk. And they did not repent of their murders or their sorceries or their sexual immorality or their thefts" (9:20-21). Those not killed refuse to repent, that is, the rest of the human race was so hardened that "they would not change their minds" (Smith). By this time, one-half of the population of the earth has been destroyed, and many have been tormented for five months, but they still do not turn to the Lord. Consequently, vices will reign in the place of virtues (Smith). They will worship demons and idols (Deut. 32:17; 1 Cor. 10:20) and as a result, they will commit murder, sorceries, and sexual immorality.

Conclusion: In response to the prayers of persecuted saints, God pours out judgment, including demons, to torment and even kill a third of the world's population, but those remaining will not repent, even though God has mercifully spared them.

In the Trumpet judgments, God will use demons to judge. That may sound shocking to us, but a reflection on the Scripture will reveal that it is not as unusual as it may appear. The Old Testament declares that the wrath of man shall praise God (Ps. 76:10). God used Pharaoh and Judas to accomplish His purposes. Paul instructed the Corinthians to deliver a believer to Satan "for the destruction of the flesh" (1 Cor. 5:5). Paul said of himself, "lest I should be exalted above measure by the abundance of the revelations, a thorn in the flesh was given to me, a messenger of Satan to buffet me, lest I be exalted above measure" (2 Cor. 12:7). So, it should not be surprising that God will use demons to judge.

The Trumpet judgments are at the end of the second half of the Great Tribulation. They emerge from the seventh seal, last for five months, and go up to the Second Coming.

Interlude

The Little Book "I saw still another mighty angel coming down from heaven, clothed with a cloud. And a rainbow was on his head, his face was like the sun, and his feet like pillars of fire" (10:1). The word "another" implies that a different mighty angel was mentioned before this one. In Revelation 5:2, there is a strong angel. The Greek word rendered "strong" in Revelation 5:2 is the same as that translated "mighty" in this passage. Thus, the other mighty angel is the one in Revelation 5:2 (Smith; Morris). The description of the angel shows that the mighty angel "came straight from the presence of God and the risen Christ" (Barclay). Thus, the cloud denotes that he is a heavenly messenger, the rainbow that the One who commissioned him is faithful, and the sun reflects the glory of the One he represents.

"He had a little book open in his hand" (10:2a). John does not reveal the contents of this little book. It is probably Revelation 11:1-13.

"And he set his right foot on the sea and his left foot on the land, and cried with a loud voice, as when a lion roars. When he cried out, seven thunders uttered their voices" (10:2b-3). The posture of the angel denotes his "colossal size" and his mission to the world. The message of the angel is universal; it concerns all on the sea and land (Morris). Hence, John sees a mighty angel with a little book and hears a thundering message. What was the message he heard?

"Now when the seven thunders uttered their voices, I was about to write; but I heard a voice from heaven saying to me, 'Seal up the things which the seven thunders uttered, and do not write them'" (10:4). In Revelation 1:19, John was told to write what he saw. Every time he saw a vision, he recorded it. This time, however, an unidentified voice tells John to "seal up," that is, not disclose (Mounce) what the seven thunders said and not to write down what he heard.

The Seven Trumpets

"The angel whom I saw standing on the sea and on the land raised up his hand to heaven and swore by Him who lives forever and ever, who created heaven and the things that are in it, the earth and the things that are in it, and the sea and the things that are in it, that there should be delay no longer, but in the days of the sounding of the seventh angel, when he is about to sound, the mystery of God would be finished, as He declared to His servants the prophets" (10:5-7). The mighty angel announces, "There should be delay no longer." The martyrs in Revelation 6 asked, "How long, O Lord, holy and true, until You judge and avenge our blood on those who dwell on the earth?" (6:10). God has been delaying His judgments to give sinners time to repent (2 Pet. 3:1-9; Wiersbe). Now there is no more delay. God will no longer intervene to give people further opportunities to repent (Mounce). The mystery of God is the "sacred secret" about God that has not been fully revealed, but the prophets have declared it. It pertains to the establishment of the kingdom (11:15) on the earth (Walvoord).

"Then the voice which I heard from heaven spoke to me again and said, 'Go, take the little book which is open in the hand of the angel who stands on the sea and on the earth.' So I went to the angel and said to him, 'Give me the little book.' And he said to me, 'Take and eat it; and it will make your stomach bitter, but it will be as sweet as honey in your mouth'" (10:9). This is a "clear reference" to Ezekiel 3:1-3. God's revelation is bitter-sweet, "disclosing judgment as well as mercy" (Swete). As the interlude between the sixth and seventh seal was about believers, so this interlude is about the two witnesses in chapter 11. After their testimony, they are destroyed (11:7).

"Then I took the little book out of the angel's hand and ate it, and it was as sweet as honey in my mouth. But when I had eaten it, my stomach became bitter" (10:10). In ancient times, to teach a Jewish boy the alphabet, it was written on a slate of a mixture of flour and honey. The boy was told what the letters were and how they sounded. The teacher would then point at a letter and ask: "What is that and how does it sound?" If the boy answered correctly, he was allowed to lick the letter off the slate as a reward! Perhaps that is the backdrop of saying that God's Word is sweeter than honey (Barclay). Have you ever had to "eat" your words? That is an expression that means we had to retract our words in a humiliating way. Eating God's word is the opposite; it is assimilating what He said.

"And he said to me, 'You must prophesy again about many peoples, nations, tongues, and kings'" (10:11). This probably pertains to the prophecies following the seventh trumpet in Revelation 11:15 (Mounce). The prophecy concerns everyone, regardless of "racial, geographic, ethic, or social distinctions" (Mounce).

The Temple "Then, I was given a reed like a measuring rod. And the angel stood, saying, 'Rise and measure the temple of God, the altar, and those who worship there. But leave out the court which is outside the temple, and do not measure it, for it has been given to the Gentiles. And they will tread the holy city underfoot for forty-two months" (11:1-2). Measuring the Temple probably

The Seven Trumpets

suggests ownership and protection. The Greek word translated "temple" is *naos*, the building itself that included the holy place and the holy of holies. The altar is, therefore, probably the altar of incense (Smith), which stood in the holy place. There is no question about it, John says there will be a Temple on earth. God will protect the Temple, altar, and worshipers, at least in some sense. John is told *not* to measure the court of the Gentiles.

The Gentiles will tread over the Holy City, Jerusalem, for forty-two months. The time of 3½ years is "derived" from Daniel 7:25. In Revelation 11, 12, and 13, three "time" designations appear 1) forty-two months (11:2; 13:5), 2) 1260 days (11:3; 12:6) and 3) time, times, and half a time (12:14). These three-time descriptions are each referring to three and one-half years. During these 3½ years, the Temple will be given to the Gentiles (11:2), the Antichrist will reign (13:5), the two witnesses will minister (11:3), and Israel will flee into the wilderness (12:6, 12:14). These 3½ years are the 3½ years before the coming of Christ (Mt. 24:15-30). That indicates that the interlude is a flashback.

Two Witnesses "And I will give power to my two witnesses, and they will prophesy one thousand two hundred and sixty days prophesy one thousand two hundred and sixty days, clothed in sackcloth. These are the two olive trees and the two lampstands standing before the God of the earth" (11:3-4). The time of their ministry is given as "one thousand two hundred and sixty days," that is 3½ years (see comment on 11:2), the same amount of time that the Holy city is said to be tread underfoot (Swete). The two witnesses are "the two olive trees and the two lampstands," figures that allude to Zechariah 4:2-3. In Zechariah, the two olive trees are prophets (Zech. 4:3)

"And if anyone wants to harm them, fire proceeds from their mouth and devours their enemies. And if anyone wants to harm them, he must be killed in this manner. These have power to shut heaven, so that no rain falls in the days of their prophecy; and they have power over waters to turn them to blood, and to strike the earth with all plagues, as often as they desire" (11:5-6). Any attempt to destroy the two witnesses brings destruction. They also have authority and power over the earth.

"When they finish their testimony, the beast that ascends out of the bottomless pit will make war against them, overcome them, and kill them. And their dead bodies will lie in the street of the great city which spiritually is called Sodom and Egypt, where also our Lord was crucified. Then those from the peoples, tribes, tongues, and nations will see their dead bodies three-and-a-half days, and not allow their dead bodies to be put into graves. And those who dwell on the earth will rejoice over them, make merry, and send gifts to one another, because these two prophets tormented those who dwell on the earth" (11:7-10). The beast is Satan (Walvoord, who says that the beast out of the sea in chapter 13 is the world dictator and the beast out of the land in chapter 13 is the false religious leader), or at least of "demonic origin." Spiritually, Jerusalem will be like Sodom and Egypt. "The sum total of humanity dwelling on the earth" (Smith) will see the corpses of the two witnesses. The party is because the two witnesses "tormented" earth dwellers with plagues such as drought

The Seven Trumpets

and turning rivers into blood (11:6).

"Now, after the three-and-a-half days, the breath of life from God entered them, and they stood on their feet, and great fear fell on those who saw them. And they heard a loud voice from heaven saying to them, 'Come up here.' And they ascended to heaven in a cloud, and their enemies saw them. In the same hour, there was a great earthquake, and a tenth of the city fell. In the earthquake, seven thousand people were killed, and the rest were afraid and gave glory to the God of heaven" (11:11-13). The message of the witnesses did not move them to faith, but the resurrection of the witnesses moved them to fear. The ascension of the two witnesses is not fulfilled in the rapture because the rapture will occur in a moment, whereas the two witnesses ascend gradually.

"The second woe is past. Behold, the third woe is coming quickly" (11:14). The second woe is the sixth trumpet. At this point in the book, it is past (9:13-21) and there has been an interlude (10:1-11:13). The third woe, the seventh trumpet, is now coming "without further delay" (Swete).

Summary: The sweet/bitter message that John was to deliver to the whole world was that during the Great Tribulation, the Temple in Jerusalem will be desecrated, but two witnesses with great power will be killed, resurrected, and translated to heaven.

The Seventh Trumpet

The Seventh Trumpet "Then the seventh angel sounded: And there were loud voices in heaven, saying, 'The kingdoms of this world have become the kingdoms of our Lord and of His Christ, and He shall reign forever and ever!'" (11:15). The seventh trumpet is the glorious announcement that the Lord will take over the kingdoms of this world and reign forever. Christ will rule on the earth for one thousand years, and God's kingdom will "in some sense continue in the new heaven and the new earth" (Walvoord).

The Twenty-Four Elders "And the twenty-four elders who sat before God on their thrones fell on their faces and worshiped God, saying: 'We give You thanks, O Lord God Almighty, The One who is and who was and who is to come, Because You have taken Your great power and reigned'" (11:16-17). The twenty-four elders represent the church (see comment on 4:9-10). The elders worshiped God as Creator (4:10-11), praised Christ as Redeemer (5:9-10), and now thank God and Christ (11:15) for their reign. Moreover, Wiersbe has suggested that in this passage, the elders thank God that Christ reigns supremely (11:17), that God judges righteously (11:18), and that He rewards graciously (11:18).

God Judges "The nations were angry, and Your wrath has come, and the time of the dead, that they should be judged" (11:18a). When the two witnesses were killed, the nations rejoiced (11:9-10). Now they are angry because they can't get their way. They are angry with God (Ps. 2:1-3). Who are the dead, and when will they be judged? Some say this is the judgment of the wicked dead at the Great White Throne Judgment (Smith; Mounce; Wiersbe). It has also been said that the judgment of the dead refers to the resurrection of the righteous dead, since the wicked dead are not raised until after the millennium (Walvoord).

God Rewards "And that You should reward Your servants the prophets and the saints, and those who fear Your name, small and great" (11:18b). God will reward the prophets, a group that at least includes the prophets of the Tribulation. The two witnesses are called prophets (11:3, 6, 10). The prophets are rewarded for their service, for they are now called not only prophets but also servants (see also 7:3). The saints comprise the rest of the believers, excluding the prophets. They are probably faithful believers of the Tribulation. The last description may be an explanation of the two groups: they are the ones who fear God, both the small and the great. The reward will be reigning with the Lord in the kingdom (2:25-27).

God Destroys The elders conclude with "and should destroy those who destroy the earth" (11:18c). Those who destroy the earth are "those living on the earth at the time who rebel against God" (Walvoord). H. H. Farmer said, "If you go against the grain of the universe, you get splinters."

The Temple "Then the temple of God was opened in heaven, and the ark of His covenant was seen in His temple. And there were lightnings, noises, thunderings, an earthquake, and great hail" (11:19). God reveals His Temple and Ark of the Covenant at the very last, which represents His mercy. The "mercy seat" was on the Ark of the Covenant. Nevertheless, this scene is also accompanied by "lightnings, noises, thunderings, an earthquake, and great hail," which could indicate judgment. Barclay says that this scene means that the glory of God will be "fully displayed," which "is a terrifying threat to the enemies of God, but an uplifting promise to the people of God's covenant." God will fully display His glory, that is, He will display His justice in judging sinners and His mercy in saving sinners.

Summary: In the end, God will judge the world, reward the saints, and reign forever.

Chapter 7

THE EXPLANATORY PROPHECIES

The Dragon "Now a great sign appeared in heaven: a woman clothed with the sun, with the moon under her feet, and on her head a garland of twelve stars. Then being with child, she cried out in labor and in pain to give birth" (12:1-2). The woman represents Israel, as evidenced by the fact that her child is Christ (12:5) and she flees into the wilderness (12:6), not Egypt. The woman clothed with the sun, who has the moon under her feet and a garland of twelve stars on her head, is "plainly" an allusion to Genesis 37:9 (Smith). In Genesis, the sun and the moon represent Jacob and Rachel, Joseph's mother and father. The stars represent the sons of Jacob. Thus, the woman is Israel, and the twelve stars are the twelve tribes of Israel, though the symbolism "may extend beyond this to represent in some sense the glory of Israel and her ultimate triumph over her enemies" (Walvoord). The labor and pains have been taken as a reference to the "sufferings of Israel as a nation" (Walvoord).

"And another sign appeared in heaven: behold, a great, fiery red dragon having seven heads and ten horns, and seven diadems on his heads. His tail drew a third of the stars of heaven and threw them to the earth. And the dragon stood before the woman who was ready to give birth, to devour her Child as soon as it was born" (12:3-4). The dragon is a sign that points to Satan (12:9). His red color denotes his "murderous purpose" (Smith; Walvoord; Mounce). He has "seven heads and ten horns and seven diadems." Daniel saw a beast with ten horns, which is often interpreted as the Roman Empire (Dan. 7:7). However, what takes place here actually occurs three and a half years before the coming of Christ (12:6, 14). Thus, the ten horns represent the *revived* Roman Empire (Walvoord). The fact that Satan has ten horns "represents his power over the kingdoms of the world" (Swete). The stars are symbols of the Devil's angels, that is, demons (Smith; see 12:9; 1:20).

"She bore a male Child who was to rule all nations with a rod of iron. And her Child was caught up to God and His throne" (12:5). Obviously, the Child is Jesus Christ (Swete), who, as Psalm 2:9 says, will rule with a rod of iron (see 19:15). In the meantime, He has ascended into heaven (Smith). In other words, the dragon's attempt to devour the Child failed.

"Then the woman fled into the wilderness, where she has a place prepared by God, that they should feed her there one thousand two hundred and sixty days" (12:6). What is being described is the time just before Christ returns. This flight will take place in the middle of the seven years of the Tribulation, that is, at the beginning of the Great Tribulation (see Mt. 24:15). The amount of time that the woman is in the wilderness is the same

The Explanatory Prophecies

amount of time for the ministry of the two witnesses of chapter 11, namely three and a half years (see comment on 11:2). Santa is behind anti-semitism.

"And war broke out in heaven: Michael and his angels fought with the dragon; and the dragon and his angels fought, but they did not prevail, nor was a place found for them in heaven any longer. So the great dragon was cast out, that serpent of old, called the Devil and Satan, who deceives the whole world; he was cast to the earth, and his angels were cast out with him" (12:7-9). This is a fulfillment of Daniel 12:1 (Smith; Walvoord) and is "nothing less than a supreme attempt on the part of the Dragon to unseat the woman's Son and to re-establish himself in the Presence of God" (Swete; Mounce). The dragon's attack not only failed, but it also resulted in expulsion from heaven (Swete).

"Then I heard a loud voice saying in heaven, 'Now salvation, and strength, and the kingdom of our God, and the power of His Christ have come, for the accuser of our brethren, who accused them before our God day and night, has been cast down.' And they overcame him by the blood of the Lamb and by the word of their testimony, and they did not love their lives to the death. 'Therefore rejoice, O heavens, and you who dwell in them! Woe to the inhabitants of the earth and the sea! For the devil has come down to you, having great wrath, because he knows that he has a short time'" (12:10-12). The expulsion of Satan from heaven results in praise in heaven and a pronouncement of woe for those on the earth. Here, salvation is not deliverance from the penalty of sin (Walvoord). Instead, it is primarily delivered from the constant accusation of the dragon. They overcame the devil "by trusting in the atoning merits of the blood and holding to the word of their testimony, i.e., they publicly declared their faith even in the face of death" (Smith).

The point of this portion of the chapter seems to be that Satan will pursue Israel even more vigorously after he is thrown out of heaven (12:13).

"Now when the dragon saw that he had been cast to the earth, he persecuted the woman who gave birth to the male Child" (12:13). Satan persecutes Israel to thwart God's work (Walvoord).

"But the woman was given two wings of a great eagle, that she might fly into the wilderness to her place, where she is nourished for a time and times and half a time, from the presence of the serpent" (12:14). This statement brings the reader back to the same event described in verse 6. God's protection program will last three and a half years, the length of the last half of the Tribulation, that is, the Great Tribulation (see comment on 11:2; also Smith).

"So the serpent spewed water out of his mouth like a flood after the woman, that he might cause her to be carried away by the flood. But the earth helped the woman, and the earth opened its mouth and swallowed up the flood which the dragon had spewed out of his mouth" (12:15-16). Satan will attempt to destroy Israel, but God will protect her. The flood may be literal water (Zech. 14:5; Smith) or it may be symbolic (see "like a flood") of a force design to destroy the fugitives (Smith; Walvoord). Walvoord concludes that whether by natural or supernatural means, God will preserve a godly remnant, "though according to Zechariah

The Explanatory Prophecies

13:8, two-thirds of Israel in the land will perish."

"And the dragon was enraged with the woman, and he went to make war with the rest of her offspring, who keep the commandments of God and have the testimony of Jesus Christ" (12:17). The dragon is angry at Israel because he failed to destroy her. So, now he makes war with the rest of her seed (Smith). The expression "make war" denotes "prolong conflict" (Smith). The "rest of her offspring" are faithful believers (Smith argues that the term "the rest" refers to "those Israelites who do not live in Judea;" Walvoord disagrees, saying that they are Jewish believers).

To sum up, in the middle of the Tribulation, Satan will be thrown out of heaven and will attempt to destroy Israel and believers for three and a half years.

The Scripture has much to say about the Antichrist and his activities, much more than can be covered in a short compass. Revelation 13:1-10, however, gives an overview of his activities. This chapter has been called "the center and the essence of the whole book" (Barclay).

The Antichrist "Then I stood on the sand of the sea. And I saw a beast rising up out of the sea, having seven heads and ten horns, and on his horns ten crowns, and on his heads a blasphemous name" (13:1). Mounce points out that in the ancient world the sea was associate with evil and points to Revelation 11:7 and 17:8 where the beast is said to come from the abyss.

The seventh head and the ten horns do not align with any historical events (see below). Moreover, the beast from the sea in Revelation 13 reigns for three and a half years before Christ returns (13:5). Therefore, the beast of Revelation 13:1 is a future form of the Roman Empire, specifically the *revived* Roman Empire (Walvoord).

Later, John says that "the seven heads are seven mountains" (17:9) and "there are also seven kings. Five have fallen, one is, and the other has not yet come" (17:10). In other words, according to Revelation 17, the seven heads are "not contemporaneous, but successive" (Smith; Walvoord), the last one is "not yet come." So, the seven heads represent the heads of the Roman Empire, one of which has not yet emerged. The one that has not yet come is the head of the revived Roman Empire, the Antichrist.

If the fourth beast of Daniel 7 is the Roman Empire, the ten horns are a problem because historically, the Roman Empire did not have ten kings. The only way to interpret the ten kings as literal rulers of the Roman Empire is to conclude that they have not yet reigned; they are still in the future. In Daniel 7, the ten horns exist at the end of time and are part of the revived Roman Empire. The ten horns in Revelation 13 are kings who had not yet received their power in John's day but would go along with the beast (17:11-12). The time when they and the beast would appear is when they made war with the Lamb (17:14), which means when Christ returns. So, just before the Second Coming, the Roman Empire will be restored and have ten kings (Walvoord, "The Prophecy of The Ten-Nation Confederacy," pp. 99-105).

"Now the beast which I saw was like a leopard, his feet were like the feet of a bear, and his mouth like the mouth of a lion. The dragon gave him his power, his throne, and great authority"

The Explanatory Prophecies

(13:2). These animals represent swiftness (leopard), strength (bear), and strong speaking ability ("roar of a lion). The revived Roman Empire will have these characteristics. The dragon, that is, Satan (12:9), is the one who will give the beast "his power, his throne, and great authority" (13:2).

In chapter 12, the dragon has "seven heads and ten horns, and seven diadems on his head" (12:3) and the beast of chapter 13 has "seven heads and ten horns, and on his horns ten crowns" (13:2). The beast has his horns crowned, not his heads, but the point is that the beast of the sea is identified with the dragon. The dragon works through the beast "as his agent" (Swete). Satan does not conduct his work openly; instead, he operates through people (Morris). Satan will be the power behind the revived Roman Empire.

"And I saw one of his heads as if it had been mortally wounded, and his deadly wound was healed" (13:3a). Later in the chapter, it is said that the *beast* is "wounded by the sword and lived" (13:14). The wounding of one of the heads as the death of the Roman Empire and the healing as the revived Roman Empire in the Tribulation before the return of Christ (Walvoord; also Alford).

This verse is critical for understanding the passage. The passage begins with a description of the beast, including the revised Roman Empire (13:1-2). Then, Revelation 13:3 speaks of one of the *heads* of the beast *as if* it is wounded, but Revelation 13:14 indicates that it is the *beast* that is wounded. So, is verse 3 talking about the empire or one of the heads?

In Daniel 7, the beast represents "kings" (Dan. 7:17) and yet "kingdoms" (Dan. 7:23; see Smith). The kingdom expresses itself through its head, which represents the kingdom as being wounded to death; the Roman Empire is dead. It is the *empire* that will be given life again (13:14); the Roman Empire will be revived. At the same time, the revived Roman Empire will have a head, the Antichrist. In Revelation 13:3, "One of the heads" is a reference to the emperor who is "not yet come" (17:10; Smith). In that the Roman Empire will have life again (13:14) and have a head again (13:3), it will be *as if* the head were wounded and healed. As Mounce points out, "the text does not say that the *head* was restored."

In the remainder of this passage, through verse 10, the beast, which according to Daniel can represent the king (Dan. 7:17) or the kingdom (Dan. 7:23), is a reference to the king, that is, the Antichrist.

"And all the world marveled and followed the beast" (13:3b). Perhaps the wonderment of the world will be at the reestablishment of the Roman Empire. At least part of the reason for the world's wonder is explained in verse 13.

To sum up, the Roman Empire will be revived. The revived form will have ten horns, that is, ten kingdoms. According to Daniel 7, another little horn will conquer three of these. That little horn is the Antichrist. The Antichrist will arise from the revived Roman Empire. The Antichrist will head the revived Roman Empire, a United States of Europe and, at the beginning of the Tribulation, make a covenant with Israel (Dan. 7:27). The world will follow the Antichrist.

The Explanatory Prophecies

"So they worshiped the dragon who gave authority to the beast; and they worshiped the beast, saying, 'Who is like the beast? Who is able to make war with him?'" (13:4). The Antichrist will go to war. In its worship of the beast, the admiring world is, in fact, worshiping the evil power behind the beast (Swete). Satan wants to be worshiped (Mt. 4:8-10).

"And he was given a mouth speaking great things and blasphemies, and he was given authority to continue for forty-two months. Then he opened his mouth in blasphemy against God, to blaspheme His name, His tabernacle, and those who dwell in heaven" (13:5-6). This alludes to the little horn of Daniel 7 (Swete; Mounce). According to Daniel, the little horn, another name for the Antichrist, will have "a mouth speaking pompous words" (Dan. 7:8, 20) and shall "speak pompous words against the Most High" (Dan. 7:25). Another passage describing the Antichrist says of him that he "shall do according to his own will: he shall exalt and magnify himself above every god, shall speak blasphemies against the God of gods" (Dan. 11:36). Paul says of him, "who opposes and exalts himself above all that is called God or that is worshiped so that he sits as God in the temple of God, showing himself that he is God" (2 Thess. 2:4).

His authority continues for forty-two months, that is, three and a half years (see 11:2), the length of the Great Tribulation (Walvoord). The duration of the Antichrist's reign has been determined by God, not by the beast or Satan, a thought that will encourage the saints (Morris).

"It was granted to him to make war with the saints and to overcome them. And authority was given him over every tribe, tongue, and nation" (13:7). The Antichrist will be "granted" permission to make war. He will only function by divine permission (Morris). He will be a world dictator.

"All who dwell on the earth will worship him, whose names have not been written in the Book of Life of the Lamb slain from the foundation of the world" (13:8). Except for the saints, all earth-dwellers will worship the Antichrist. Much more will be said about this religious system later in the book (17:1-18). For now, suffice it to say the world will be deceived.

"If anyone has an ear, let him hear" (13:9). At the end of each of the letters to the seven churches, the Lord says, "He who has an ear, let him hear what the Spirit says to the churches." Here, "what the Spirit says to the churches" is omitted, implying that the church is no longer on the earth (Smith, p. 64). The contemporary equivalent is "Now hear this!" (Mounce).

"He who leads into captivity shall go into captivity; he who kills with the sword must be killed with the sword. Here is the patience and the faith of the saints" (13:10). Apparently, this is an allusion to such passages as Jeremiah 15:2, 43:11. Those who persecute the saints will, in turn, suffer the righteous wrath of God, which should serve as a warning to the persecutors and as an encouragement to the saints (Walvoord).

To sum up, since the Antichrist, who will do horrible things, will be destroyed, trust and endure.

The Explanatory Prophecies

God allows this "to continue for forty-two months" (13:5). God determines the time and it is short. God "granted to him to make war with the saints and to overcome them" (13:7). Without God's permission, the Antichrist would not be able to do anything. God will destroy the Antichrist (13:10). The Antichrist will be thrown into the lake of fire (19:20).

The False Prophet "Then I saw another beast coming up out of the earth, and he had two horns like a lamb and spoke like a dragon" (13:11). The first beast came out of the sea (13:1) and the second out of the land. His coming out of the earth indicates that he is a creature of the earth rather than heaven (Walvoord). Speaking like a dragon means that he is "motivated by the power of Satan," who is the dragon (12:9).

"And he exercises all the authority of the first beast in his presence, and causes the earth and those who dwell in it to worship the first beast, whose deadly wound was healed" (13:12). Earlier it was said that the whole world worshiped the Antichrist (13:8). Now it is revealed that the False Prophet is the one who causes the world to do that. The first beast fights the battles of the dragon and the second beast supports the first with power derived from the dragon. The business of the second is to promote the worship of the first (Swete).

"He performs great signs, so that he even makes fire come down from heaven on the earth in the sight of men. And he deceives those who dwell on the earth by those signs which he was granted to do in the sight of the beast, telling those who dwell on the earth to make an image to the beast who was wounded by the sword and lived" (13:13-14). The False Prophet will deceive the world (13:14) by performing miracles (13:13) and by giving an image of the beast power to speak (13:14). He will simulate the miracles performed by true prophets (Ex. 7:11 ff.; Swete). Like Satan (12:9), the False Prophet will deceive. The miracles he can perform will be the means of deception.

Then, the False Prophet will get the world to make an image of the beast, which was wounded and comes to life. The wound by the sword refers to the decline of the Roman Empire and "did live" refers to its revival. The Antichrist is "the symbol of this miraculous restoration" (Walvoord). This image is mentioned three times in this chapter and seven times in the chapters that follow (14:9, 11; 15:2; 16:2; 19:20; 20:4). It will be the focus and the focal point of the false worship (Walvoord).

"He was granted power to give breath to the image of the beast, that the image of the beast should both speak and cause as many as would not worship the image of the beast to be killed" (13:15). The False Prophet will be given the power to make the image breathe. The False Prophet does not provide the image of life. That is "solely the prerogative of the Godhead" (Smith). The image will appear to manifest life through breathing, but it will likely be nothing more than a robot (Walvoord). The False Prophet will give the image power to speak. A ventriloquist makes the image say that all who refuse worship to the image should be put to death.

"He causes all, both small and great, rich and poor, free and slave, to receive a mark on their right hand or on their foreheads,

The Explanatory Prophecies

and that no one may buy or sell except one who has the mark or the name of the beast, or the number of his name" (13:16-17). The False Prophet will get people to worship the Antichrist by controlling the economy.

"Here is wisdom. Let him who has understanding calculate the number of the beast, for it is the number of a man: His number is 666" (13:18). How is it possible to calculate the number of a name? In the ancient world, letters of the alphabet were used as numbers. The Roman numeral system assigns letters a numeric value: I = 1, V = 5, X = 10, L = 50, C = 100, and M = 1000. If that were done with the English alphabet, A would stand for one, B for two, C for three, etc. (Barclay). Thus, every name could be translated into numbers that could be calculated.

To sum up, the False Prophet will cause the earth to worship the Antichrist by performing miracles, threatening death, and controlling the world's economy.

One Hundred and Forty-Four Thousand "Then I looked, and behold, a Lamb standing on Mount Zion, and with Him one hundred and forty-four thousand, having His Father's name written on their foreheads" (14:1). This is a picture of the Lamb standing on Mount Zion with the one hundred and forty-four thousand after His Second Coming at the beginning of the millennium.

"And I heard a voice from heaven, like the voice of many waters, and like the voice of loud thunder. And I heard the sound of harpists playing their harps. They sang as it were a new song before the throne, before the four living creatures, and the elders; and no one could learn that song except the hundred and forty-four thousand who were redeemed from the earth" (14:2-3). In chapter 5, the elders sang a new song (5:9-10). This is different because only the 144,000 could learn it. The elders sang about being redeemed and ruling with the Lord. The song here probably concerns being protected throughout the Tribulation.

"These are the ones who were not defiled with women, for they are virgins. These are the ones who follow the Lamb wherever He goes. These were redeemed from among men, being first fruits to God and to the Lamb. And in their mouth was found no deceit, for they are without fault before the throne of God" (14:4-5). They are virgins. They are free from spiritual adultery (Walvoord; Mounce). They were not spiritually defiled with beast worship. Rather than worship the beast, they worshiped the Lamb. They are the first fruits of "all Israel," which will be saved (Smith).

The Everlasting Gospel "Then I saw another angel flying in the midst of heaven, having the everlasting gospel to preach to those who dwell on the earth; to every nation, tribe, tongue, and people; saying with a loud voice, 'Fear God and give glory to Him, for the hour of His judgment has come; and worship Him who made heaven and earth, the sea and springs of water'" (14:6-7). It is not the gospel of grace, nor the gospel of the kingdom, but the announcement of the judgment of God and the command to worship Him (Walvoord). The message is all should fear God.

Babylon is Judged "And another angel followed, saying, 'Babylon is fallen, is fallen, that great city, because she has made all nations drink of the wine of the wrath of her fornication'" (14:8). The first angel announces that judgment has come; the

The Explanatory Prophecies

next two angels get specific. This one proclaims that Babylon has fallen. Babylon is an actual city because it is mentioned in connection with other real cities, not symbolic cities (16:19). This view argues that prophecies concerning Babylon in the Old Testament have not been fulfilled. Therefore, Babylon will be rebuilt. More specifically, the Old Testament predicted that Babylon would be destroyed entirely and not inhabited (Isa. 13:19-22; Jer. 51:24-26; 61-64), that Babylon would be suddenly destroyed (Jer. 51:8), and that Babylon would be destroyed in the Day of the Lord (Isa. 13:6, 9-11). When Babylon fell, however, it was not completely destroyed and left uninhabited. It was not destroyed for hundreds of years after the empire fell (Walvoord on 18:8-9), and, of course, it was not destroyed on the Day of the Lord, which is still in the future.

Revelation 17:5 says that Babylon is a mystery, indicating that Babylon in that passage is not to be taken literally (Smith on 17:5) and the meaning "is not open and obvious to all" (Morris). Therefore, in Revelation 17:5, Babylon is used in some figurative sense. Also, in Revelation 17, Babylon is portrayed as a harlot (17:1-5) who is guilty of fornication (17:2), which is used figuratively in the Bible of spiritual unfaithfulness. Babylon is a false religious system. Thus, in the Bible, Babylon is a city, a political, commercial world empire (renowned for its luxury; see Mounce on 14:8), and it stands for a system of false religion. Wall Street is an illustration of a name being used literally and figuratively. It is a place and a system.

Which way is "Babylon" being used in Revelation 14:8? Most interpret the Babylon symbol as a reference to Rome, either in a political sense (Mounce) and/or a religious sense (Smith), or figuratively as the "overthrow of all the evil Babylon stands for" (Morris). Walvoord argues that religious Babylon will be destroyed in the middle of the Tribulation and the city of Babylon will be destroyed at the end of the Tribulation (16:19). Therefore since the context of Revelation 14 is the end of the Tribulation, the Babylon of Revelation 14:8 is the literal, rebuilt city of Babylon.

The reason for the judgment of Babylon is that she "made all the nations drink of the wine of the wrath of her fornication." The expression "the wine of the wrath of her fornication" is probably a shortened combination of "the wine of the wrath of God" (14:10) and "the wine of her fornication" (17:2; Walvoord). What Babylon dispensed was fornication, that is, unfaithfulness to God (Isa. 1:21), which is described as wine and wrath. From the participants' point of view at the time, it was wine, but from God's point of view, it was wrath. The nations are made drunk with the wine of fornication (17:4), "on which account the wrath of God comes upon them" (Smith).

Beast worshipers are Judged "Then a third angel followed them, saying with a loud voice, 'If anyone worships the beast and his image, and receives his mark on his forehead or on his hand, he himself shall also drink of the wine of the wrath of God, which is poured out full strength into the cup of His indignation'" (14:9-10a). The Greek word translated "full strength" means "unmixed," referring to the practice of diluting wine with water (Mounce). The

The Explanatory Prophecies

wine they drink is "unmixed," that is, untempered, by the mercy and grace of God" (Walvoord). The wrath of God in the Tribulation is not eternal. It is just a cup full (16:19-20).

"He shall be tormented with fire and brimstone in the presence of the holy angels and in the presence of the Lamb. And the smoke of their torment ascends forever and ever; and they have no rest day or night, who worship the beast and his image, and whoever receives the mark of his name" (14:10b-11). The torment of the trumpet judgments was temporary; the final form will be "without time-limits" (Swete). "Forever and ever" is literally "into the ages of ages." It is used for God's existence (Smith).

Those who *do not* worship the beast are killed (13:15). Those who *do not* take the mark of the beast cannot buy and sell (13:17). Those who *do* worship the beast and *do* take the mark of the beast (14:10) suffer the worst fate. They experience the wrath of God and endure eternal torment (Mounce).

Saints will be Blessed "Here is the patience of the saints; here are those who keep the commandments of God and the faith of Jesus. Then I heard a voice from heaven saying to me, 'Write: 'Blessed are the dead who die in the Lord from now on.' 'Yes,' says the Spirit, 'that they may rest from their labors, and their works follow them'" (14:12-13). In spite of the threat of the False Prophet, some will refuse to worship the beast and receive the mark of the beast and, as a result, will die as martyrs and will be rewarded. It is better to reign with Christ forever than with the beast for three and a half years.

The Riddle of Revelation

The Earth will be Judged "Then, I looked, and behold, a white cloud, and on the cloud sat One like the Son of Man, having on His head a golden crown, and in His hand a sharp sickle. And another angel came out of the temple, crying with a loud voice to Him who sat on the cloud, 'Thrust in Your sickle and reap, for the time has come for You to reap, for the harvest of the earth is ripe.' So He who sat on the cloud thrust in His sickle on the earth, and the earth was reaped" (14:14-16). Is the Son of Man Jesus Christ? God the Father has committed all judgment to the Son (Jn. 5:22) because He is the Son of Man (Jn. 5:27). The point is "the precise moment has come for reaping and there must be no further delay" (Swete).

"Then another angel came out of the temple which is in heaven, he also having a sharp sickle. And another angel came out from the altar, who had power over fire, and he cried with a loud cry to him who had the sharp sickle, saying, 'Thrust in your sharp sickle and gather the clusters of the vine of the earth, for her grapes are fully ripe.' So the angel thrust his sickle into the earth and gathered the vine of the earth, and threw it into the great winepress of the wrath of God. and the winepress was trampled outside the city, and blood came out of the winepress, up to the horses' bridles, for one thousand six hundred furlongs" (14:17-20). A second picture of judgment is given. The second follows the first, as the grapes harvest follows the wheat harvest (Swete). This time, an *angel* comes from the presence of God with a sharp sickle. In John's day, grapes were put in a trough and trampled by foot (Mounce). In the Scripture, grape treading was used to

The Explanatory Prophecies

illustrate Divine wrath (Isa. 63:3; Joel 3:15; Rev. 19:15).

The winepress in this passage is located outside the city, and it is no doubt a reference to the city of Jerusalem (Sweet; Smith; Mounce). This refers to the battle of Armageddon in the valley of Jehoshaphat (Isa. 63:3; Jer. 25:30-31; Joel 3:13b-16a; Smith). This is fulfilled in Revelation 19:15 (Walvoord; Mounce). The point is the "finality of the blow" (Swete).

The last part of the verse poses two problems: distance and depth. The distance of one thousand six hundred furlongs is approximately 200 miles (Mounce and Morris say 184 miles). The holy land is only 160 miles from north to south. Some attempt to explain it as a literal distance, saying that the land is approximately 200 miles (Walvoord) or that the Lord will rearrange the contour of the region to fulfill this prophecy (Isa. 2:21; Smith). Most interpret it symbolically.

The second problem is the depth of blood "up to the horses' bridles" for 200 miles. To come as close as possible to a literal fulfillment, it has been said that this is "simply as a literal spattering of blood" (Walvoord). This is also often taken symbolically.

These measurements are hyperbole. The blood flows deep and extends the length and breadth of the land (Mounce). There will be a complete judgment of the whole earth and the destruction of all wicked (Morris).

What is the difference between these two harvests? Some have suggested that the first is the harvest of saints and the second is the harvest of sinners (Swete). Others argue that the first harvest represents judgment in general, and the second is the final, climactic one (Alford; Walvoord).

Summary: God's justice will triumph because even though some saints will be protected and some martyred now, later, all the world will be judged and the saints will be rewarded.

Vernon Grounds, the President of a theological seminary, recounts a story about a janitor he met while he was a seminary student. The janitor let Grounds and other students play basketball in the gym. While they played, the janitor read. One day, the students asked him what he was reading and the janitor said, "The Book of Revelation." These theological students had just had a course in Revelation, so they thought they would explain the book to this uneducated janitor. They asked, "Do you understand the book?" He replied, "Yes. It is saying that Jesus is going to win."

Chapter 8

THE SEVEN BOWLS

The Seven Bowl Judgments	15:1-16:21
1. Prelude (in heaven)	15:1-8
2. Six Bowl Judgments	16:1-14
3. Interlude	16:15
4. Seventh Bowl Judgments	16:16-21

Prelude

The Wrath of God "Then I saw another sign in heaven, great and marvelous: seven angels having the seven last plagues, for in them the wrath of God is complete" (15:1). The bowl judgments are the *last* plagues (15:1, 6, 8; 16:9, 21), implying that all the judgments in Revelation are plagues (Smith; Walvoord) and that these are the final judgments before the coming of Christ (Walvoord). These plagues complete God's wrath. The Greek word rendered "complete" means "having reached its end, complete, finished." When the seventh bowl is poured out, a loud voice comes "out of the temple of heaven, from the throne, saying, 'It is done!'" (16:17). The plagues complete the wrath of God.

The Riddle of Revelation

The Victorious Saints "And I saw something like a sea of glass mingled with fire, and those who have the victory over the beast, over his image and over his mark and over the number of his name, standing on the sea of glass, having harps of God" (15:2). In chapter 4, John saw "before the throne, there was a sea of glass, like crystal" (4:6). Here he sees "something like a sea of glass" and this time it is "mingled with fire." The sea of glass is probably a symbol of God's holiness (see comment on 4:6). Since the fire denotes judgment (Walvoord; Barclay), these judgments issue from a holy God (Smith). Those who have had victory over the beast, his image, mark, and number (in other words, the Antichrist) are standing on the sea of glass with harps. These are the saints the Antichrist martyred. They were victorious because they remained faithful unto death instead of receiving the mark of the beast (Walvoord).

The Songs of the Saints "They sing the song of Moses, the servant of God, and the song of the Lamb, saying: 'Great and marvelous are Your works, Lord God Almighty! Just and true are Your ways, O King of the saints! Who shall not fear You, O Lord, and glorify Your name? For You alone are holy. For all nations shall come and worship before You, for Your judgments have been manifested'" (15:3-4). The victorious saints sing. The song of Moses was sung at every Sabbath evening service in the synagogue (Barclay). The second song is the song of the Lamb. The song of the Lamb is the song of redemption from sin because of the sacrifice of the Lamb of God.

The Seven Angels "After these things I looked, and behold, the

The Seven Bowls

temple of the tabernacle of the testimony in heaven was opened. And out of the temple came the seven angels having the seven plagues, clothed in pure bright linen, and having their chests girded with golden bands" (15:5-6). The seven angels with the seven last plagues come from the very presence of God (Mounce).

The Four Living Creatures "Then one of the four living creatures gave to the seven angels seven golden bowls full of the wrath of God who lives forever and ever. The temple was filled with smoke from the glory of God and from His power, and no one was able to enter the temple till the seven plagues of the seven angels were completed" (15:7-8). In Revelation 5:8, the golden bowls were full of incense, representing the prayers of the saints. Now, golden bowls are filled with the wrath of God. Since these are the only two references to golden bowls in Revelation, it may be suggested that the judgment is in response to the prayers of the saints (Mounce). In fact, the judgments are an answer to prayer for justice. The fifth seal judgment reveals that martyrs from the Tribulation pray for justice. (6:9-11). God answers those prayers for justice by pouring out the seven trumpet judgments on the earth (8:3-6; 9:13-14). In Revelation 14, there may be another indication that judgment during the Tribulation is an answer to the prayers of the martyrs for justice (14:18). All seven bowl judgments are an answer to prayer for justice (15:7-8; 16:6-7).

The first four trumpet judgments only affect a third of the earth, while the bowl judgments have "no such limitation (Swete); they are universal and greater in intensity (Walvoord). So, while there is much similarity between the trumpet judgments and the bowl judgment, "similarities do not prove identity" (Walvoord).

Six Bowls

The First Bowl "Then I heard a loud voice from the temple saying to the seven angels, "Go and pour out the bowls of the wrath of God on the earth. So the first went and poured out his bowl upon the earth, and a foul and loathsome sore came upon the men who had the mark of the beast and those who worshiped his image" (16:1-2). The fact that the first bowl judgment falls on those who have the mark of the beast and worship his image indicates that the pouring out of the bowl judgments will take place *after* the middle of the Tribulation (Walvoord). It is in the middle of the Tribulation that the Antichrist comes to power. It will take "considerable time" after that for the False Prophet to perform miracles and get the world to make the image and it appears the reception of the mark of the beast and the worship of the Antichrist become widespread when the first bowl is released. The bowls come at the end of the Tribulation (Smith). The fact that this judgment falls on those who have the mark of the beast and worship his image also implies that there will be those living who had not received the mark and worship the Antichrist (Smith).

The Second Bowl "Then the second angel poured out his bowl on the sea, and it became blood as of a dead man; and every living creature in the sea died" (16:3). The sea becomes the tomb of all creatures that live in it.

The Third Bowl "Then the third angel poured out his bowl

The Seven Bowls

on the rivers and springs of water, and they became blood. And I heard the angel of the waters saying: 'You are righteous, O Lord, The One who is and who was and who is to be, because You have judged these things. For they have shed the blood of saints and prophets, and You have given them blood to drink. For it is their just due. And I heard another from the altar saying, 'Even so, Lord God Almighty, true and righteous are Your judgments'" (16:4-7). In the third trumpet judgment, a third part of the water is turned to wormwood, whereas here, the whole supply is turned into blood. The eternal God is righteous to judge. They shed the blood of the saints and their blood will be shed.

The Fourth Bowl "Then the fourth angel poured out his bowl on the sun, and power was given to him to scorch men with fire. And men were scorched with great heat, and they blasphemed the name of God who has power over these plagues; and they did not repent and give Him glory" (16:8-9). The Greek text reads "the" men, indicating that the ones scorched are the ones who received the mark and worshiped the Antichrist (16:2). These judgments are directed at the image worshipers (Smith).

The Fifth Bowl "Then the fifth angel poured out his bowl on the throne of the beast, and his kingdom became full of darkness; and they gnawed their tongues because of the pain. They blasphemed the God of heaven because of their pains and their sores, and did not repent of their deeds" (16:10-11). The fifth trumpet judgment (9:1-2) and the fifth bowl judgment are darkness. Instead of darkness over one country or for a third of a day, it is over the throne and kingdom of the Antichrist. The previous plagues fell on the subjects of the empire. This one is directed at the seat of the empire, the throne of the beast, that is, the Antichrist. As the judgments intensify, so does the refusal of people to repent (see 8:7; 9:20-21; 16:9, 11, 21; Mounce, p. 184). They did not repent, that is, change their minds concerning their deeds. What are the deeds? The text here does not say. In chapter 9, it is stated that they did not repent of idolatry and immorality (9:20-21). In Revelation 16, it is stated that they did not repent and give God glory (16:9) and blasphemed God (16:11). Within the context of this section of the book, their deeds, at the very least, include idolatry, worshiping the beast, and blaspheming God. Like Pharaoh, they hardened their hearts in the midst of terrible suffering (Smith).

The Sixth Bowl "Then the sixth angel poured out his bowl on the great river Euphrates, and its water was dried up, so that the way of the kings from the east might be prepared. And I saw three unclean spirits like frogs coming out of the mouth of the dragon, out of the mouth of the beast, and out of the mouth of the False Prophet. For they are spirits of demons, performing signs, which go out to the kings of the earth and of the whole world, to gather them to the battle of that great day of God Almighty" (16:12-14). The wrath of God (16:1) in the form of demonic activity is dispatched. Like the sixth trumpet judgment (9:14), the sixth bowl judgment involves the Euphrates River. There is a difference. This time, the water is dried up. Like the second Egyptian plague (Ex. 8:5), frogs are mentioned. Here, words are like frogs. Although the name of the river is not mentioned, the Euphrates River is dried up (Isa. 11:15; Zech. 10:11) so that the kings of the East can move westward (Walvoord). According to the ancient historian Herodotus, the city of Babylon fell when the waters of the Euphrates River, which ran through the city, were diverted and the "the last obstacle to its fall" was removed (Swete).

Who are the kings (plural) of the East? There have been as many as fifty different interpretations (Walvoord), including Japan (Smith) and China. Gog, the king of the North, was destroyed earlier (Ez. 38:3, 15).

Unclean spirits come out of the mouth of the unholy Trinity. The unclean spirits are demons (16:14). The dragon is Satan (12:9). The beast is the Antichrist (13:1-10) and the False Prophet is the second beast of Revelation 13:11 (Swete). This is the first time, but not the last, that the second beast is called the False Prophet (19:20; 20:10).

The comparison to frogs may be a reference to uncleanness. Leviticus says, "All in the seas or in the rivers that do not have fins and scales, all that move in the water or any living thing which is in the water, they are an abomination to you" (Lev. 11:10). In other words, frogs were unclean animals. Perhaps there is also a reference to their croaking (Mounce).

The rulers of the "whole world" (Mounce) are motivated by demons, working through the words ("by deceit," Mounce) of the unholy trinity, and gather together for the battle of that great day of God Almighty. This is the gathering of the armies for the battle described in Revelation 19:19. The sixth bowl is not the battle itself; rather, it places armies on the battlefield (Swete).

The Greek word translated "battle" means "war." Some argue that there is another word for battle; therefore, what is referred to here is a war, a series of battles. This is the climax of a series of battles described in Daniel 11:40-45. The nations gather together to fight each other, but when Christ returns, they turn to fight Him. This is the great battle of God Almighty, in which God's omnipotence will be fully demonstrated (Walvoord).

When they gather together, God says, "Behold, I am coming as a thief. Blessed is he who watches, and keeps his garments, lest he walk naked and they see his shame" (16:15). Coming as a thief indicates that the coming is sudden, unexpected, and results in a loss (Walvoord). All who are not ready suffer loss. Those who are ready, having watched and kept themselves, will be blessed. "Coming as a thief looks back to Jesus' warning to believers to be vigilant because of the unexpected timing of His return (Mt. 24:43-44)" (*NKJV Study Bible*).

The image used to describe the gain or the loss is clothing. The garments have been taken literally, that is, as a reference to nudism (Smith) and as a symbol of salvation, but this is something that they do. Therefore, this refers to the righteousness of the saint (see 19:8; Walvoord). These are the saints who did not take the mark of the beast and who were not martyred; they were hiding (Mt. 24:16; Walvoord).

The Seventh Bowl "And they gathered them together to the place called in Hebrew, Armageddon" (16:16). The Greek word translated "Armageddon" means "mount of Megiddo," which overlooks the plain of Megiddo (Smith) to the east and the valley

The Seven Bowls

of Esdraelon to the northeast (Walvoord). The fourteen-by-twenty-mile valley of Esdraelon cannot hold the armies of the world. This, then, must be the central point of a military engagement involving armies that span a two-hundred-mile area (14:20), including Jerusalem (Zech. 14:1-3; Walvoord).

What is the relationship between the sixth trumpet and the sixth bowl? Both concern the Euphrates River. Do the bowls parallel the trumpets, or do they follow them? Walvoord says the sixth trumpet is the early stages of the invasion, with a statement of their ultimate purpose and the sixth bowl being the actual fulfillment. The time difference is in days rather than months or years.

"Then the seventh angel poured out his bowl into the air, and a loud voice came out of the temple of heaven, from the throne, saying, 'It is done!'" (16:17). The wrath of God (16:1) in the form of air pollution is disseminated. Like the seventh Egyptian plague (Ex. 9:22), and the seventh trumpet (11:19), the seventh bowl involves hail. The final bowl plague affects the air. This plague has "wider significance than the smiting of the earth, the sea, the freshwater, and even the sun" (Swete). The air affects health and life (Swete). Control of the air and space is crucial in military matters (Walvoord). Citing Ezekiel 38:9, 16, Smith says that "the allusion to air travel seems to be beyond question." "It is done" fulfills Revelation 10:7 (Smith).

"And there were noises and thunderings and lightnings; and there was a great earthquake, such a mighty and great earthquake as had not occurred since men were on the earth" (16:18). At the end of the seals (8:5) and at the end of the trumpets (11:9), there is a similar refrain, indicating that each series of judgments ends at the close of the Tribulation and that the lighting and thunder in each case are intended as an omen of the judgment about to come (Smith). Because of the similarity of the seventh judgment in each of the three sets of judgments, they must overlap and all three conclude at the end of the Tribulation.

This earthquake is greater than any previous earthquake! There are six literal earthquakes recorded in the Bible: 1) Mt. Sinai (Moses and Israel after the Exodus in the Wilderness), 2) Mt. Horeb (Elijah's cave experience, 1 Kings 19:11), 3) During the reign of Uzziah (Amos 1:1), 4) At the time of the Crucifixion (Mt. 27:51), 5) At the time of the Resurrection of Christ (Mt. 28:2), 6) That which freed Paul and Silas from prison (Acts 16:26). Isaiah mentions earthquakes as being a form of judgment that God sometimes uses (Isa. 29:6). The Book of Revelation predicts many to come in the last days (Rev. 8:5; 11:13; 16:18).

Every year, 500,000 detectable seismic or micro-seismic disturbances occur worldwide. Of these, 100,000 can be felt, and 1,000 can destroy either lives or property. Worse in intensity: Alaska, 1964. It was 8.9 on the Richter scale–equivalent to an explosion 100 times greater than a nuclear bomb of 10,000 megatons. Worst loss of life: In 1556, 830,000 died in China. In 1976, in Peking, 650,000 died and 780,000 were injured. In the U.S., more than 70 million people live in high-to-moderate-risk regions. Highest risk areas: San Francisco, Los Angeles, Memphis, Salt Lake City, Seattle, Anchorage, Alaska, and Charleston, S.C.

The Seven Bowls

"Now the great city was divided into three parts, and the cities of the nations fell. And great Babylon was remembered before God, to give her the cup of the wine of the fierceness of His wrath" (16:19). Which city is "the great city?" Since Jerusalem is referred to as the "great city" in Revelation 11:8, some argue that it is Jerusalem (Smith). Jerusalem has topographical changes at the Second Coming (Zech. 14:4), but Jerusalem is not entirely destroyed (Walvoord). Others take it as Rome (Swete; Mounce). It may be the rebuilt city of Babylon (see comments on 14:8; Walvoord). Babylon is split into three parts, a picture of awesome destruction (Walvoord). Other Gentile cities also fall. The wrath of God is poured out on Babylon.

"Then every island fled away, and the mountains were not found. And great hail from heaven fell upon men, each hailstone about the weight of a talent. Men blasphemed God because of the plague of the hail, since that plague was exceedingly great" (16:20-21). Not only Babylon but the topography of the entire world is affected. This is no local plague; it is worldwide (Swete). The whole earth is radically changed. Revelation 6:14 says, "Every mountain and island was moved out of its place." Revelation 16:20 inverts the order, but the fact that it is the same event indicates that the time here is parallel with Revelation 6:14, namely, the close of the Tribulation (Smith).

A talent varied in weight in different periods of history. It represented what a normal man could carry, approximately 100 pounds (Walvoord, Sweet, and Smith say about 114 pounds). Hail that size would kill anyone hit by it (Swete). The earthquake, no doubt, caused widespread destruction and loss of life; hail further damaged some structures that had survived the earthquake (Walvoord). "The mills of God, if they grind slowly, are never stopped except by human repentance" (Swete; Jer. 37:24?).

Throughout this chapter, there is a progression in their blasphemy. They blasphemed the name of God (16:9) and the God of heaven (16:11), whom they may have conceived as being "an absentee God" (Smith). Now they blaspheme God. They now, if not before, recognize that it is God, but they still are stubbornly unrepentant. The time has come to destroy the destroyer.

Summary: As the bowls of the last plagues of God's wrath are poured out on the earth, men blaspheme God, but God is just in His judgment because men martyred the saints.

The trumpet and bowl judgments "fall in rapid succession like trip-hammer blows" (Walvoord, p. 232). The indication that the bowl judgments are poured in rapid succession is that the sores of the first bowl are still felt during the fifth plague (Mounce p. 292). I've learned that life is like a roll of toilet paper. The closer it gets to the end, the faster it goes.

God is just to judge (16:5-7). He is gracious, giving people the opportunity to repent (16:9, 11), but people don't repent. They do not heed the warnings (16:9, 11).

God is just to bless (Heb. 6:10-12). What do I have to do to be blessed? The references to being blessed in Revelation tell us. "Blessed is he who reads and those who hear the words of this

The Seven Bowls

prophecy, and keep those things which are written in it; for the time is near" (1:3). Those who keep the word are those who not only hear but also do what this book says to do. They do not hear and forget, nor do they hear and neglect. They hear and "keep," that is, "obey from the heart.

"Here is the patience of the saints; here are those who keep the commandments of God and the faith of Jesus. Then I heard a voice from heaven saying to me, 'Write: 'Blessed are the dead who die in the Lord from now on.' 'Yes,' says the Spirit, that they may rest from their labors, and their works follow them'" (14:12-13). Saints who endure (Grek: "patience," "endurance"), obey (they keep the commandments of God), and rely on the Lord (They have faith in Jesus) will be blessed. Their works follow them, which indicates they will be rewarded (1 Cor. 3:11-15).

"Behold, I am coming as a thief. Blessed is he who watches and keeps his garments, lest he walk naked and they see his shame" (16:15). "Then he said to me, 'Write: 'Blessed are those who are called to the Marriage Supper of the Lamb!'" (19:9). The Marriage Supper of the Lamb indicates that being blessed includes being rewarded.

Some saints will not heed the warning; they will be ashamed (1 Jn. 2:28). We will appear before the Lord naked (no acts of righteousness, no works), with some clothes (some acts of righteousness, some works), or well-dressed. It would be like meeting the Lord just as you stepped out of the shower, naked, or meeting Him dressed in rags, or meeting Him at the front door well-dressed.

The Riddle of Revelation

Some sinners and some saints do not heed the warning. Years ago, Robert Cyr, national director of Operation Lifesaver, an organization in Canada seeking to decrease accidents between cars and trains, said, "Studies have shown that when people hear a train whistle, their minds tell them to accelerate the speed." About 43% of the accidents occur at railroad crossings equipped with flashing lights, bells, or gates. Cyr also said that many drivers "even have the audacity to drive around or under gates" (*Our Daily Bread*, April 6, 1991).

There is a psychological phenomenon called normalcy bias. Normalcy bias refers to our natural tendency to revert to normalcy when facing a crisis. It causes people to underestimate the possibility of a disaster. People believe that something that has *never happened before will never happen*. People have a hard time preparing for and dealing with something that has never occurred.

In his book *Wealth, War, and Wisdom*, Barton Biggs says, "By the end of 1935, 100,000 Jews had left Germany, but 450,000 still remained. Wealthy Jewish families continued to think and hope that the worst was over. "Many of the German Jews, brilliant, cultured, and cosmopolitan as they were, were too complacent. They had been in Germany so long and were so well-established that they couldn't believe there was going to be a crisis that would endanger them. They were too comfortable. They believe the Nazi's anti-semitism was an episodic event and that Hitler's bark was worse than his bite. (They) reacted sluggishly to the rise of Hitler for completely understandable but tragically erroneous reasons. Events moved much faster than they could have imagined."

Chapter 9

CONCLUSION

Unraveling The Riddle of Revelation begins with recognizing that Revelation 19 refers to the Second Coming of Christ, and Revelation 4-18 immediately precedes the Second Coming of Christ. The period immediately preceding the Second Coming of Christ is commonly referred to as the Tribulation. Since it is described in several other passages of Scripture, understanding what those passages say is helpful in understanding the book of Revelation.

Daniel 9 predicts a seven-year period before the establishment of the kingdom (the 70th week of Daniel). This is the period commonly called the Tribulation. Daniel 9 is the only passage in the Bible that says the Tribulation period will last for seven years. Daniel 9 also outlines the Tribulation. At the beginning of the Tribulation, the Antichrist will make a covenant with Israel and, in the middle of the Tribulation, he will break the covenant with an Abomination of Desolation.

Matthew 24 also describes the Tribulation. That is evident by the fact that, after an overview of the period, Jesus explicitly states that He is referring to the Abomination of Desolation spoken of by the prophet Daniel (Mt. 24:15). Matthew 24 fills in many of the details of the Tribulation that is only outlined in Daniel 9. It gives the characteristics of the Tribulation from beginning to end (Mt. 24:4-14), refers to the middle of the Tribulation (Mt. 24:15) and describes some of the characteristics of the second half of the Tribulation, which Jesus calls the "Great Tribulation" (Mt. 24:21). He then teaches that immediately after the Tribulation He will returned to set up His Kingdom.

1. False Christ (Mt. 24:4-5)
2. War (Mt. 24:6-7a)
3. Famines (Mt. 24:7b)
4. Pestilences and earthquakes (Mt. 24:7c)
5. Martyrdom (Mt. 24:9-13)
6. The middle of the Tribulation begins the Great Tribulation (Mt. 24:15-28)
7. Cosmic disturbances come before His Second Coming (Mt. 24:29)
8. Christ returns to set up His kingdom (Mt. 24:30, 25:31).

The overall outline of the book of Revelation is given in Revelation 1:19. John is told to write about the things that he sees (Rev. 1), the things that are (Rev. 2-3), and the things that will be after that (Revelation 4-22). Revelation 4-22 describes the seals, trumpets, and bowls. The first four seals of Revelation 6 parallel the description of the beginning of the Tribulation in Matthew 24. If the first four signs in Matthew 24 are in the first half of the Tribulation and are parallel to the first seal, the first four seals are

Conclusion

in the first half of the Tribulation.

Characteristic	Matthew 24 Beginning of Sorrows	Revelation 6 Four Horsemen
False Christ	Matthew 24:4-5	Revelation 6:1-2
War	Matthew 24:6-7a	Revelation 6:3-4
Famine	Matthew 24:7b	Revelation 6:5-6
Death	Matthew 24:7c	Revelation 6:7-8

The Structure of Revelation 4-16

Seals (4:1-8:1)
    Prelude (4:1-5:14)
        1st Seal (6:1-2): The Antichrist will be Revealed
        2nd Seal (6:3-4): War will be Released
        3rd Seal (6:5-6): Famine will Result
        4th Seal (6:7-8): Death will Reign
        5th Seal (6:9-11): Martyrdom will Reoccur
        6th Seal (6:12-17): Natural Disaster will run Wild
        Sealed Servants on Earth (7:1-8)
        Serving Saints from the Great Tribulation in Heaven (7:9-17)
        7th Seal (8:1): The Trumpet Judgments are coming

Trumpets (8:2-11:19)
    Prelude (8:2-6)
        1st Trumpet (8:7): A Hail and Fire Storm will come
        2nd Trumpet (8:8-9): The Ocean will be Affected
        3rd Trumpet (8:10-11): Fresh Water will be Affected
        4th Trumpet (8:12-13): Darkness will come
        5th Trumpet (9:1-12): Demonic Locusts will come from the Pit

6th Trumpet (9:13-21): Demonic Hordes come from the East
Little Book is a Bitter and Sweet Message (10:1-11)
The Temple (11:1-2)
Two Witnesses (11:3-14)
7th Trumpet (11:15-19): God will Judge the World
Explanatory prophecies (12:1-17)
The Dragon (12:1-17)
The Antichrist (13:1-10)
The False Prophet (13:11-18)
The 144,000 (14:1-5)
The Eternal Gospel (14:6-7)
Babylon will be Judged (14:8)
Beast Worshippers will be Judged (14:9-11)
Saints will be Blessed (14:12-13)
The Earth will be Judged (14:14-20)
The Bowls (15:1-16:21)
Prelude (15:1-16:1)
1st Bowl (16:2): Sores on those with the mark of the beast
2nd Bowl (16:3): All sea creatures died
3rd Bowl (16:4-7): Rivers and springs become blood
4th Bowl (16:8-9): The sun scorches those with the mark of the beast
5th Bowl (16:10-11): The kingdom of the beast blasphemes the name of God
6th Bowl (16:12-16): The Euphrates River is dried up
The Lord Returns (16:15)
7th Bowl (16:16-21): the battle of Armageddon

Appendix I

SEALS, TRUMPETS, & BOWLS

Not everyone agrees with the solution to The Riddle of Revelation that has been presented so far. Not even those who believe that the fulfillment of Revelation is still future and that Revelation 4-18 describes the Tribulation agree with this solution. The disagreement concerns the relationship between the three series of judgments and the Tribulation. Here is a summary of the various views, including the one that has already been presented.

The Seals are in the First Half

Explanation Some say the seal judgments are in the first half of the Tribulation. Dwight Pentecost claims the seals fall upon the earth in the first portion of the Tribulation, and they will continue through the period (Pentecost, *Things to Come*, pp. 360-361). "The trumpets began in the middle of the Tribulation and depict events during the entire second half of the Tribulation. The bowl judgments cover a brief period at the end of the Tribulation just before the second coming of Christ (Pentecost, *Things to Come*, p. 363; Johnson, Constable, McGee, and Criswell).

The Riddle of Revelation

| Seals | Trumpets | Bowls |

Evaluation This arrangement ignores the fact that all three series of judgments end at the coming of Christ (*cf.* Mt. 24:29 with 6:13-14, 11:15, 16:17).

The Seals and the Trumpets are in the First Half

Explanation Some put the seal and the trumpet judgments in the first half of the Tribulation. One version of this approach maintains a strict, continuous chronology throughout the book. It says that the seal and the trumpet judgments occur in the first half of the Tribulation (4:1-11:19) and that the middle of the Tribulation occurs when Satan is cast out of heaven (12:1-17). The bowl judgments are in the second half of the Tribulation (13:1-18:24). Not all forms of this interpretation divide the book that way, but all variations place the seal and trumpets judgments in the first half of the Tribulation (Larkin, *The Book of Revelation*, 1919, pp. 14-15; David Cooper, *An Exposition of the Book of Revelation*, p. 16). Tim La Haye and Tom Ice place the middle of the Tribulation between Revelation 14:20 and 15:1. The seal, trumpet judgments, and prophecy in 12:1-14:20 occur in the first half of the Tribulation. Warren Wiersbe says the first three and a half years are covered in Revelation 6-9, the middle of the Tribulation in Revelation 10-14 and the last three and half years in Revelation 15-19 (Wiersbe, *Be Victorious*, p. 61). Later, he says, "The trumpet judgments are

Appendix I: Seals, Trumpets, & Bowls

released during the last half of the Tribulation and the bowl judgments during the last half" (Wiersbe, p. 73).

Seals	Trumpets	Bowls

Evaluation This arrangement ignores the fact that all three series of judgments end at the coming of Christ (*cf.* Mt. 24:29 with Rev. 6:13-14; 11:15; 16:17). Alford notes that any system of interpretation that requires the sixth seal to belong to any other time than the great day of the Lord "stands ... self-condemned" (Alford, vol. IV, p. 249).

The Seals and the Trumpets are in the Last Half

Explanation Some claim the seal, trumpet, and bowl judgments are all in the last half of the Tribulation. This is a recapitulation approach to the book.

Walvoord says, "There is a remarkable similarity between the progress of chapter 6 as a whole and the description given by our Lord of the end of the age in Matthew 24:4-31. In both passages the order is (1) war (Matt. 24:6-7; Rev. 6:3-4), (2) famine (Matt. 24:7; Rev. 6:5-6), (3) death (Matt. 24:7-9; Rev. 6:7-8), (4) martyrdom (Matt. 24:9–10, 16–22; Rev. 6:9–11), (5) the sun darkened, the moon darkened, and the stars falling (Matt. 24:29; Rev. 6:12-14), (6) a time of divine judgment (Matt. 24:32—25:26; Rev. 6;15-17). The general features of Matthew 24 are obviously quite parallel to the events of the book of Revelation beginning in chapter 6" (Walvoord, p. 123).

| | |Seals Trumpets Bowls| |

Evaluation The advantage of this arrangement is that it acknowledges the fact that all three series of judgments extend to the end of the Tribulation. It does not account for the expression "the beginning of sorrows" in Matthew 24:8 and the fact that there are only four horsemen in Revelation 6.

The Seals cover both Halves

Explanation Some insist the seal judgments are an overview of both halves of the Tribulation. The trumpet judgments cover the second half and the bowl judgments occur at the very end of the Tribulation. The support for this view is: 1) Each series of judgments ends at the Second Coming of Christ (*cf.* Mt. 24:29 with 6:13-14; 11:15; 16:17). 2) Revelation 6:14 says, "Every mountain and island was moved out of its place" and, while Revelation 16:20 inverts the order, the fact that it is the same event indicates that the time here is parallel with Revelation 6:14, namely the close of the Tribulation (see Mark Bailey, "The Tribulation" in *The Road to Armageddon*, p. 71; James M. Gray, *Synthetic Bible Studies*, p. 334; Wilbur M. Smith, *Moody Monthly*, 58:49; W. K. Harrison, *Bib Sac*, 115:203).

Appendix I: Seals, Trumpets, & Bowls

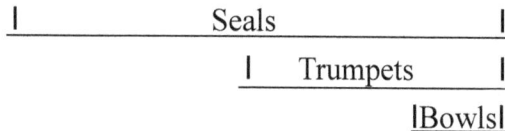

Evaluation This arrangement solves the last piece of The Riddle of Revelation.

Summary: Even among those who believe that the Revelation describes the Tribulation, there is disagreement about where the middle of the Tribulation takes place in the book of Revelation. The list of views is not exhaustive. C. I. Scofield says Matthew 24:4-14 has a double interpretation: 1) It describes the present age. 2) It also describes Daniel's 70th week. Lewis Sperry Chafer holds that Matthew 24:4-8 describes the present church age, which takes place before the beginning of the 70th week of Daniel. Matthew 24:9-26 describes the Great Tribulation (Chafer, *Systematic Theology*, vol., pp. 120-121).

Appendix II

MATTHEW 24 AND THE SEALS, TRUMPETS, & BOWLS

This chart illustrates the connection between Matthew 24 and the seals, trumpets, and bowls of Revelation. The parallel between Matthew 24 and the seals of Revelation 6 is unmistakable. There are clear parallels between Matthew 24 and the trumpets of Revelation; however, Revelation provides more detailed information about the trumpets than Matthew 24. Both, however, refer to the coming kingdom. Matthew 24 does not mention what is contained in the bowls of Revelation, except that both Matthew 24 and Revelation refer to the end of the Tribulation.

Matthew 24, The Seals, Trumpets, and Bowls

Matthew 24	Seals/Rev. 6	Trumpets/Rev. 8-9	Bowls/Rev. 16
False Christ (24:4-5)	Antichrist revealed (6:2)		
War (24:6)	War released (6:3-4)		
Famines (24:7:a)	Famine results (6:5-6)		
Pestilence and Earthquakes (24:7b)	Death reigns (6:7-8) ¼ killed with sword, hunger, and beast		

The Riddle of Revelation

Martyrdom (24:9-13)	Martyrdomre occurs (6:9-11)		
Worldwide preaching (24:14)	Great multitudes saved (7:1-11)		
Great Tribulation (24:21)		Hail and fire (8:7) 1/3 trees/ all grass	
		Sea turns to blood (8:8-9) 1/3 sea life/ships	
		Rivers turn bitter (8:10-11) 1/3 bitter/death	
		Sun gets dark (8:12-13) 1/3 darkness	
		demonic locusts (9:1-12) torment for 5 months	
		demonic hordes Euphrates (9:13-21) 1/3 killed (now 50%) No repentance	
			Sores distributed (16:1-2) all w/mark
			Blood dispensed (16:3) All sea life died
			Blood delivered (16:4-7) Rivers
			Heat descends (16:8-9) Sun. No repentance
			Darkness dispersed (16:10-11) throne of beast No repentance
			Euphrates demonic activity dispatched. (16:12-16) Armageddon
Cosmic disturbances (24:29) darkness Sun, moon, stars Matthew 25:31	Cosmic disturbances (6:12-14) darkness sun, moon, stars island, mts		Pollution disseminated wrath is Done (16: 17-21) island, mts, hail
		Kingdom (11:18-19)	

BIBLIOGRAPHY

Abbott-Smith, G. *A Manuel Greek Lexicon of the New Testament.* Edinburgh: T & T Clark, 1960 (reprint of the 1937 edition).

Andersen, Sir Robert. *The Coming Prince.* Grand Rapids: Kregel Publications, 1984.

Alford, Henry. *The Greek New Testament.* Revised by Everett F. Harrison. Chicago: Moody Press, 1958.

Archer, Jr., Gleason L. *A Survey of the Old Testament Introduction.* Chicago: Moody, 1974.

Arndt, William and Gingrich, F. Wilbur, translated by Walter Bauer. *A Greek-English Lexicon of the New Testament and Other Early Christian Literature.* Chicago: The University of Chicago Press. 1979.

Bailey, Mark. "The Tribulation" in *The Road to Armageddon.* Charles R. Swindoll, John F. Walvoord, J. Pentecost. Nashville: Thomas Nelson, 1999.

Barclay, William. *The Revelation of John.* Philadelphia: The Westminster Press, 1976.

Boutflower, Charles. *In and Around the Book of Daniel.* Grand Rapids: Zondervan Publishing House, 1963.

Burrows, *Millar. Burrows on the Dead Sea Scrolls: An Omnibus of Two Famous Volumes: The Dead Sea Scrolls / More Light on the Dead Sea Scrolls.* Grand Rapids: Baker Book House, 1978.

Chafer, Lewis Sperry, *Systematic Theology*. Dallas: Dallas Theological Seminary, 1948.

Constable, Thomas, "Dr. Constable's Expository (Bible Study) Notes." Available at http://www.soniclight.com/constable/notes.htm.

Cooper, David L. *Future Events Revealed*. Los Angeles: Biblical Research Society, 1935.

Dana and Mantey, *A Manual Grammar of the Greek New Testament*. New York: Macmillan, 1958.

Harrison, Norman B. *The End. Rethinking the Revelation*. Minneapolis: The Harrison Service, 1941.

Hodges, Zane. "1 Thessalonians 5:1-11 and the Rapture," *Chafer Theological Seminary Journal* 6 (October–December 2000).

Ice, Thomas. "Matthew 24:31: Rapture Or Second Coming?" Modified on Oct. 10, 2016. https://www.Raptureready.com/2015/04/10/matthew-2431-Rapture-or-second-coming-by-thomas-ice/

Milligan, George. *St. Paul's Epistles to the Thessalonians*. Evangelical Masterworks series. Reprint ed. Old Tappan, N.J.: Fleming H. Revell, Co., n.d.

Morris, Leon. The Revelation of St. John. Tyndale New Testament Commentary series. Reprint ed., Leicester, England: Inter-Varsity Press, and Grand Rapids: Wm. B. Eerdmans Publishing Co., 1984.

Mounce, Robert H. *The Book of Revelation*. New International Commentary on the New Testament series. Grand Rapids: William B. Eerdmans Publishing Co., 1983.

Bibliography

Pentecost, J. Dwight. *Things to Come*, Findley, Ohio: Dunham Publishing Company, 1958.

Reese, Alexander. *The Approaching Advent of Christ*. London: Morgan & Scott, 1937

Ryrie, Charles C. *What You Need to Know About the Rapture*. Eugene, Oregon: Harvest House Publishers, 2024.

Showers, Renald E. *The Most High God: A Commentary On The Book Of Daniel*. Bellmawr, New Jersey: The Friends of Israel Gospel Ministry, Inc. 1982.

Smith, J. B., *A Revelation of Jesus Christ*. Scottdale, Pa.: Herald, 1961.

Stanton, Gerald B. *Kept from the Hour*. Grand Rapids: Zondervan Publishing House, 1956.

Swete, Henry Barclay. *The Apocalypse of St. John*. London: Macmillan Publishers Ltd, 1906.

Thiessen, Henry Clarence. *Introduction to the New Testament*. Grand Rapids, Eerdmans Publishing Company, 1943.

Van Kampen, Robert. *The Basics*. Wheaton, Ill. Crossway Books, 1993.

Van Kampen, Robert. *The Rapture Question Answered*. Grand Rapids: Fleming H. Revell, 1997.

Walvoord, John F. *The Revelation of Jesus Christ*. Chicago, IL: Moody Press, 1966. Wiersbe, Warren. *Be Victorious*. Wheaton: Victor Books, 1985.

Wood, Leon. *A Commentary on Daniel*. Grand Rapids: Regency Reference Library, 1973.

About The Author

G. Michael Cocoris is a gifted communicator. He can make even complicated subjects simple, clear, and practical. His breadth of experience has allowed him to relate to a wide range of audiences.

Michael received a Bachelor of Arts degree from Tennessee Temple University, a Master of Theology degree from Dallas Seminary, and a Doctorate of Divinity from Biola University. He traveled the United States for over a dozen years as a speaker. He has also been a seminary professor, visiting lecturer, and world traveler, including hosting tours to Israel and China.

Michael has pastored three churches, including a rural church when he was in seminary, an urban church, the historic Church of the Open Door, first in downtown Los Angeles and later in Glendora, California, and a suburban church, the Lindley Church in Tarzana California, a suburb of Los Angeles. While at the Church of Open Door, he had a daily radio broadcast.

Michael has written numerous magazine articles, mainly for *Biblical Research Monthly*. He has authored a number of books, including *Seventy Years on Hope Street, A History of the Church of the Open Door*; *How To Live A Biblical Spiritual Life*, *Clarifying the Confusion*; *Repentance, The Most Misunderstood Word in the Bible*; *Evangelism: A Biblical Approach*; *The Salvation Controversy*; *Lordship Salvation: Is It Biblical?*; *The Books of the Bible, the Subject, Structure, Situation, and Significant Verses of Each Book*; *Psalms, A Song for Every Situation, Each Summarized on One Page*; and *Counseling Theories, A Biblical Evaluation*. In addition, he was a contributor to The *NKJV Study Bible* and *Nelson's New Illustrated Bible Commentary*.

Michael is the pastor of the Lindley Church in Tarzana, California. He and his wife, Patricia, live in Santa Monica, California.

www.ingramcontent.com/pod-product-compliance
Lightning Source LLC
Chambersburg PA
CBHW070111080526
44586CB00013B/1258